100% VANCOUVER

m

100% VANCOUVER

There's so much to experience in Vancouver, where do you start? Of course you'll want to visit the beach, stroll through Gastown and do some shopping downtown or in Yaletown, but also be sure to visit Chinatown's Night Market, buy tickets for a ice hockey game in the GM Place stadium, stroll through the many galleries on South Granville, enjoy Stanley Park on rollerblades or go dancing at a trendy nightclub. This guide will take you every where you want to go in no time at all - sightseeing, shopping, culinary delights and adventure - and easy-to-use maps will show you the way.

100% VANCOUVER, EXPLORE THE CITY IN NO-TIME!

Contents

100% Easy-to-Use

To make this guidebook easy-to-use, we've divided Vancouver up into six neighborhoods and provided a detailed map for each of these areas. You can see where each of the neighborhoods lies in relation to the others on the general map in the front of the book. The letters Ⓐ to ⓩ will also let you know where to find attractions in the suburbs, hotels, and nightclubs, all described in detail later on in the guidebook.

In the six chapters that follow, you'll find detailed descriptions of what there is to do in the neighborhood, what the area's main attractions are, and where you can enjoy good food and drink, go shopping, take a walk, or just be lazy. All addresses have a number ①, and you'll find these numbers on the map at the end of each neighborhood's chapter. You can see what sort of address the number is and also where you can find the description by looking at its color:

● = sights	● = shopping
● = food & drink	● = nice to do

6 WALKS

Every chapter also has its own walk, and the maps all have a line showing you the walking route. The walk is described on the page next to the map, and it will take you past all of the most interesting spots and best places to visit in the neighborhood. You won't miss a thing. Not only will you see the most important sights, museums, and parks, but also special little shops, good places to grab lunch, and fantastic restaurants for dinner. If you don't feel like sticking to the route, you'll be able to find your way around easily with the descriptions and detailed maps.

PRICE INDICATION FOR HOTELS AND RESTAURANTS

To give you an idea of hotel and restaurant prices, you'll find an indication next to the address. The hotel prices mentioned are - unless otherwise stated - per double room per night. The restaurant prices are - unless otherwise stated - an indication of the average price of a main course.

THE RHYTHM OF VANCOUVER

Generally, Vancouver has a typically 'west coast' rhythm. People are more relaxed here and love to boast about how laid back their city is compared to Toronto, Canada's biggest city.

There is a grocery store open somewhere at pretty much any time of day. Supermarkets open early and don't close until about 11pm. Most other stores are open until 7pm most nights and until 9pm on Thursdays and Fridays.

Restaurants that serve dinner usually open at 5pm and stay open until about 11pm. Many places serve lunch as well, and often breakfast, too. Reservations are available at most restaurants, and are particularly advisable on weekends. Without reservations you'll end up waiting in line until the next table comes free. If you don't have a reservation, make sure to put your name on the waiting list as soon as you arrive.

In Vancouver, people often go out for breakfast on weekend mornings. A typical breakfast consists of eggs, toast, fried potatoes and bacon or sausages. For a lighter breakfast, try a muffin and a cup of coffee. You can get coffee in a large cardboard 'to go' cup just about anywhere, so it can be enjoyed on the way to work, while shopping or during a stroll on the beach.

August is the warmest month in Vancouver, with temperatures in the low 80s (Fahrenheit). Canadians get at least two weeks vacation a year, and most of them take time off during the summer months. In addition, British Columbia has a number of public holidays that normally fall on a Monday, resulting in a long weekend. During these public holidays, banks and offices are closed but stores are usually open.

NATIONAL PUBLIC HOLIDAYS

January 1 - New Year's Day
third Monday in May - Victoria Day
July 1 - Canada Day
first Monday in August - Civic Holiday
first Monday in September - Labor Day
second Monday in October - Thanksgiving (stores closed)
November 11 - Remembrance Day
December 25 - Christmas (stores closed)
December 26 - Boxing Day

DO YOU HAVE ANY SUGGESTIONS?

We've tried to compile this guide with the utmost care. However, the selection of shops and restaurants can change quite frequently in Vancouver. Should you no longer be able to find a certain address or have other comments or tips for us concerning this guide, please let us know. You'll find our address in the back of the book.

Hotels

Vancouver has countless hotels, from well-known large chains to small bed & breakfasts (B&Bs), and from hostels to exclusive boutique hotels. It's very easy to find an inexpensive hotel in the center of Vancouver. Prices vary between $50 and $300, but the most expensive hotels are not always the best.

In the center and outskirts of Vancouver, there are many B&Bs that are very pleasant and affordable. Booking a private room in a hostel is the cheapest way to go, but reservations are necessary as hostels are often booked months in advance. If you are looking for luxury, try either the classic Hotel Vancouver or the ultra-hip Opus.

There are a number of websites that can help in finding the perfect hotel:

- *www.vancouver.com* - the Vancouver Tourism Board's site
- *www.vancouver-hotels-1.com* - find very cheap hotels
- *www.vancouverhotelreservations.ca* - find and book Holiday Inn hotels
- *www.best-vancouver-hotels.com* - extensive information about different hotels
- *www.bbcanada.com* - for those who prefer a bed & breakfast

The selection below covers some of Vancouver's cheapest, nicest and most exceptional hotels. The letters at the hotels listed below can be found on the map at the beginning of the guide.

JERICHO BEACH HOTEL (J)

Ⓑ OPUS HOTEL

High-end

Ⓐ The **Listel Hotel** has a fantastic location in downtown Vancouver, and each of the three floors has a different theme. Works of art by local artists hang on the walls of every room on the 'gallery' and 'museum' floors and modern furniture complements the artwork well. Plus, you don't have to go far for delicious food - O'Doul's Restaurant on the ground floor serves breakfast, lunch and dinner.
1300 robson street, telephone (604) 684-8461,www.listel-vancouver.com, price from $190, bus 5 robson

Ⓑ Vancouver's hippest hotel, and the one with the most creative interior, is the **Opus** in Yaletown. The lobby contains an amazing collection of furniture in various styles, while the colorful rooms are sights to behold. Voyeurism rules here - some rooms have bathrooms with large windows overlooking the busy street. Breathe deeply... every bathroom has a oxygen sprayer, so you can inhale fresh air every 12 minutes.
322 davie street, telephone (604) 642-6787, www.opushotel.com, price from $229, skytrain stadium

Ⓒ The **Westin Bayshore** is a wonderful hotel located on the water and near Stanley Park. This hotel has more than 500 rooms and a beautiful lobby with a fireplace. Many rooms have a view of the water and most have a balcony. The décor is classic, and the beds are heavenly!
1601 bayshore drive, telephone (604) 682-3377, www.westinbayshore.com, price from $200, bus 135 stanley park

Ⓓ The oldest hotel in Vancouver, opened in 1939 by Queen Elizabeth, is the **Fairmont Hotel Vancouver**. This gorgeous building is located in the middle of the city center and the green roof figures prominently on the skyline. The Victorian interior gives the feeling of staying in an old English castle, however all the rooms are equipped with every modern convenience, including Internet access. A luxurious beauty salon downstairs is the perfect place for a little pampering.
900 west georgia street, telephone (604) 684-3131, www.hotelvancouver.com, price from $175, bus 5 robson

Mid-range

Ⓔ Near the theaters and galleries of Granville Island lies the **Granville Island Hotel**. The first thing you'll notice is an enormous terrace that is part of the hotel's bar. Rooms are spacious, many with a view of the harbor. Marble floors and Persian rugs create a lush atmosphere. The Dockside Restaurant and Pub provides a lively ambiance that fits in perfectly with Granville Island.
1253 johnston street, telephone (604) 683-7373, www.granvilleislandhotel.com, price from $150, bus 8 granville

Ⓕ The intimate atmosphere of **Mickey's Kits Beach Chalet** is ideal for romantic couples. This bed & breakfast is in a fantastic location across from Kitsilano Beach. Rooms are spacious and the serene garden, which is open to all guests, is delightful. The daily breakfast consists of muffins, croissants, eggs and fruit.
2142 west 1st avenue, telephone (604) 739-3342, www.mickeysbandb.com, price from $75, bus 2 macdonald

Ⓖ The **Delta Pinnacle Hotel** is located in a modern building with lots of glass. The bright, spacious rooms are beautifully furnished but feel a bit businesslike. Look for a table in the Showcase restaurant, however, and you're sure to be pampered. After the meal, you may have to make use of the well-equipped fitness center.
1128 west hastings, telephone (604) 684-1128, www.deltahotels.com, price from $159, bus 10 hastings

Lower-range

(H) From the outside, the **Sylvia Hotel** doesn't look inexpensive. The beautiful ivy-covered building was built in 1912. The interior, however, is simple, clean and unfussy. If you're looking for an inexpensive hotel with a good location, this is the just the place. A number of rooms have a good view of English Bay Beach and you definitely won't get bored with Stanley Park just a stone's throw away and the city center just around the corner.
1154 gilford street, telephone (604) 681-9321, www.sylviahotel.com, price from $85, bus 6 davie

(I) If you like the atmosphere of Commercial Drive, you'll like **A Place at Penny's**. The gray structure looks like an apartment building, and indeed you can rent two-room apartments here, as well as rooms containing fully equipped kitchens. The furnishings are simple, but the wood floors are distinctive.
810 commercial drive, telephone (604) 254-2229, www.pennysplacevancouver.com, price from $65, bus 10 hastings

(J) There are three hostels in Vancouver, but the **Jericho Beach Hostel** is definitely the prettiest. Located in a beautiful old military building, just minutes away from the beach, the hostel is surrounded by a field of green grass enclosed by huge trees. You can rent private rooms that sleep six, however it is advisable to reserve these well in advance.
1515 discovery street, telephone (604) 224-3208, www.hihostels.ca, price from $18, bus 4 bianca

(K) Situated on busy but pleasant Robson Street, the **Barclay Hotel** has an elegant exterior with a European feel. The rooms are simple and can sometimes be a bit noisy due to the hotel's central location.
1348 robson street, telephone (604) 688-8850, www.barclayhotel.com, price from $49, bus 5 robson

Transportation

From Vancouver International Airport you can reach the city center by taking the **Airporter Bus**. A one-way ticket costs $12 and a return ticket is $18. The bus leaves from the airport every 20 minutes and stops at several central locations in Vancouver. There are, of course, taxis readily available as well, but expect to pay about $25 for the trip to the city center. For more information, go to *wwww.yvrairporter.com* or call (604) 946-8866.

In the city center, you don't have to wait in line for **taxis** - just put your hand out. There is a standard service charge of $2.50, but on top of that the ride is generally not very expensive; $10 can take you quite far. It is customary to tip the driver a few dollars.

There are different ways to make use of public transportation in Vancouver. Unfortunately, there isn't a good subway system such as those you find in many other big cities. **Buses** are usually the easiest and cheapest form of transportation. Depending on how far you travel, a bus ticket costs about $2.50 (paid in exact change). For travel information, call Translink at (604) 953-3333 or check out *www.translink.bc.ca.*

Finally, you can also use the **skytrain** and the **seabus**. The skytrain is convenient for longer distances but doesn't have very many central stations. It is especially popular with commuters, since the route goes past many of Vancouver's suburbs. The seabus can be used to cross over to North and West Vancouver. Boats leave the downtown Waterfront Station every 15 minutes and take you to the opposite short of your choice in no time. For travel information call Translink at the number given above.

For a fun, touristy ride through the city, reserve a place on the **Vancouver trolley**. This funny red bus travels from Gastown to Stanley Park and even goes through Granville Island and Chinatown. Tickets are valid all day and allow you to get on and off where and when you like. The trolley makes a trip at 30 minute intervals.
first stop 157 water street, telephone (604) 801-5515, first bus leaves at 9am, last bus at 4pm, day card adults $26, children $13

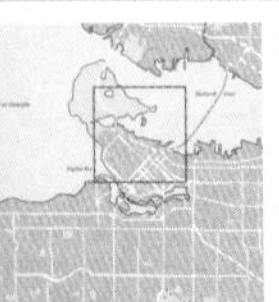

West End & Downtown

In downtown Vancouver there are many high-rise apartment buildings next to the banks, office buildings and stores. Residents here have the luxury of living and working right in the heart of the city.

West End and Downtown have pretty much grown into each other, even though the ambiance in the two parts is still quite different. With the beach and Stanley Park close by, there is always something to do in West End and the neighborhood is alive from early in the morning until late at night. The boulevard is a popular place to go skating, cycling or taking a stroll.

1

Davie and Denman Streets, on the contrary, are full of restaurants and fun shops. The residents of this area are generally students and young, working people. Furthermore, this area is home to much of the city's homosexual community and gay pride flags can be found hanging on practically every corner of Davie Street.

Downtown is always busy and offers great food, nightlife and culture. But you will notice that even the center of the city has been designed with cars in mind. Sadly, none of the streets are free of cars and even the nicest shopping avenue, Robson Street, is bisected by a four-lane road.

6 Musts!

Seawall

Rent rollerblades or bicycles and ride around

Vancouver Art Gallery

See the art or rest on the steps

Tsunami Sushi

Watch delicacies sail past in little boats

Vancouver Aquarium

Spend hours watching the river otters

Boat cruise

Cruise along English Bay and around Stanley Park

English Bay

Sunbathe on the beach

- **Sights**
- **Shopping**
- **Food & Drink**
- **Nice to do**

Sights

(7) Vancouver is not really a city known for its high-end art and culture. However, the **Vancouver Art Gallery** is an exception. The exhibitions are often excellent and the vast permanent collection includes works by Emily Carr, an artist that British Columbia is very proud of. The museum's location is beautiful as well; with huge steps leading to both entrances and a park in front, this is also a nice place to have a picnic or just to read.
750 hornby street, telephone (604) 662-4700, www.vanartgallery.bc.ca, open daily 10am-5.30pm (thu until 9pm), closed mondays in winter, entrance adults $12.50, students $8, thu evening $5, bus 5 robson

(8) Across from the Art Gallery lies **Robson Square**, with its collection of buildings designed by architect Arthur Elickson. This is a strange conglomeration of construction, with the courthouse, a waterfall and a skating rink. It's a nice place to go for a walk or to sit on the terrace of one of the underground restaurants.
800 robson street, telephone (604) 482-5600, skating rink open daily 10am-10pm, free entrance, bus 5 robson

(15) Next to busy Robson Street lies a quieter street where you can find the **Roedde House Museum**. This is a restored Victorian residence, originally built in 1893 by the architect Francis N. Rattenbury, who also designed the Vancouver Art Gallery. A visit to the Roedde house is a nice change from the hustle and bustle of downtown Vancouver.
1415 barclay street, telephone (604) 684-7040, www.roeddehouse.org, open wed-fri 2pm-4pm, sun 'tea and tour' 2pm-4pm, entrance adults $4, seniors $3, children under 12 free, reservations for group tours, bus 5 robson

⑰ **Coal Harbour**, located between downtown Vancouver and Stanley Park, was originally used to transport coal but is now a marina for yachts and sailboats. In recent years, a number of tall apartment buildings have been built, making the boulevard a bit impersonal but at the same time creating a beautiful skyline.
between nicola street and denman street on the waterfront, bus 135 stanley park

⑳ **Stanley Park** is an enormous park within a 10-minute walk of downtown. It is a huge draw for tourists, so don't plan to come here to rest. The park is surrounded by the ocean, which makes its location unique. You can enjoy cycling, walking or a visit to one of the many attractions the park has to offer.
north of the west end, free entrance, bus 135 stanley park

㉑ Some of the most famous attractions in Stanley Park are the **Totem Poles**. In actuality, the totem poles are not very old but they give a good idea of the original natives of Canada and their traditions. Every totem pole tells its own story.
brockton point in stanley park, free entrance, bus 135 stanley park

STANLEY PARK

LICENSED
MELRICHES
1993-2003
10 Years
Thank You!!
VEGGIE BURGER
Big Gooey
Cinnamon buns
made right here!
CHAI
SOYA LATTES
COFFEE BEANS

① **MELRICHES**

Food & Drink

(1) For a cup of organic coffee and an excellent breakfast sandwich, go to **Melriches**. After ordering, read the daily horoscope that is stuck to the counter every day and look for a place at the window to get a good view of the people passing by on Davie Street. Prefer to sit outside? There is an unofficial terrace in a parking lot at the back, where the owners of Melriches will be happy to put a couple of tables out for you.
1244 davie street, telephone (604) 689-5282, open mon-fri 6am-11pm, sat-sun 7am-11pm, price for coffee $1.75, bus 6 davie

(3) For those with little money but a huge appetite, don't miss **Ho Ho Fast Food**. The Chinese food here tastes best if you eat it on the beach just up the road. Choose from a large variety of dishes. The portions are large and very delicious!
1224 davie street, telephone (604) 688-9896, open daily 11.30am-11.30pm, price $5, bus 6 davie

(4) You'll probably have to wait an hour for a table if you decide to eat at **Stepho's**. This restaurant is unbelievably popular, because of its fantastic and reasonably priced Greek menu. The Greek wine and the amazing pita, made with lots of garlic, round off the meal perfectly.
1124 davie street, telephone (604) 683-2555, open daily 11.30am-11.30pm, price $9, bus 6 davie

(5) Burgers, burgers and more burgers, plus **Hamburger Mary's** has the best shakes! This kitschy restaurant, with walls covered in posters of James Dean and Marilyn Monroe, is open 20 hours a day and serves hamburgers, sandwiches or breakfasts (like scrambled eggs).
1202 davie street, telephone (604) 687-1293, open daily 7am-3am, price $8, bus 6 davie

JUPITER
CAFE
MUM'S GELA
PRICE LIST

(6) **Jupiter Café** is hip and completely relaxed. The small tables with large, comfortable chairs are an inviting sight. Try the delicious martinis and tapas and enjoy jazz, stand-up comedy, DJs or a bit of fresh air on the large terrace.
1216 bute street, telephone (604) 609-6665, open daily 4pm-1am, price $15, bus 6 davie

(10) You have to have sushi at least once while in Vancouver. This Japanese specialty was brought here by the large numbers of immigrants who came to settle in Vancouver at the beginning of the last century. At **Tsunami Sushi**, the sushi is placed on small boats that sail around the bar in a mini river. Pick out what looks good to you and pile up the empty boats; your bill will be added up at the end of your meal.
1025 robson street, telephone (604) 687-8744, open mon-thu, sun 11.30am-10.30pm, fri-sat 11.30am-11pm, price $12, bus 5 robson

(16) **Cardero's** is a good place to sit on the terrace in the middle of the day to enjoy a luscious drink, or in the evening to partake in a delicious dinner. With a view of the ocean and the yachts in the harbor, you can really experience the good life.
1583 coal harbour quay, telephone (604) 669-7666, open mon-sat 11.30am-11pm, sun 11.30am-10pm, price $18, bus 135 stanley park

(19) You don't have to know how to row in order to enjoy a beer at the **Vancouver Rowing Club**. The club building has a beautiful location and a wonderful terrace often visited by the non-rowing public.
in stanley park near coal harbour, telephone (604) 687-3400, price drink $3, bus 135 stanley park

(24) For the best Italian ice cream (made with a secret recipe), go to **Mum's Gelati**. Beachgoers have been ordering the ice cream, made fresh daily in the shop, for 25 years. You can even choose licorice flavor with real pieces of English licorice in it.
849 denman street, telephone (604) 681-1500, open daily 7.30am-10pm, price ice cream $3, bus 5 robson

(25) For something completely different try **Ukrainian Village** featuring intriguing Ukrainian specialties. The perogies are heavenly, but you can also choose between beef stroganoff and a dish made with Ukrainian sausage. The dark interior and heavy, wooden tables and chairs give it an authentic atmosphere.
815 denman street, telephone (604) 687-7440, open mon 5pm-9pm, tue-fri noon-10pm, sat 11am-10pm, sun 11am-9pm, price $12, bus 6 davie

(26) After a day at the beach, **Brass Monkey** offers an intimate ambiance and delicious food. The menu comes across as simple, but the dishes are made with great care and consequently are not cheap.
1072 denman street, telephone (604) 685-7626, open mon-fri 5pm-2am, sat 10am-3pm, 5pm-2am, sun 10am-3pm, 5pm-midnight, price $20, bus 6 davie

(27) **Banana Leaf** is great if you want an exotic treat. Try authentic Malaysian cuisine such as chicken or shellfish curries. The rice with raisins and pineapple is served in a half pineapple.
1096 denman street, telephone (604) 683-3333, open daily 11am-10.30pm, price main course $12, bus 6 davie

(30) If want to hang on to that beach house feeling, go for a drink on the roof terrace at the **Boat House Restaurant**. With a fantastic view of the boulevard, the beach and, if you're lucky, the sunset, the restaurant is famous for its fish dishes - which seem to come fresh from the nearby ocean.
1795 beach avenue, telephone (604) 669-2225, open mon-sat 11am-10pm, sun 5pm-10pm, price $20, bus 6 davie

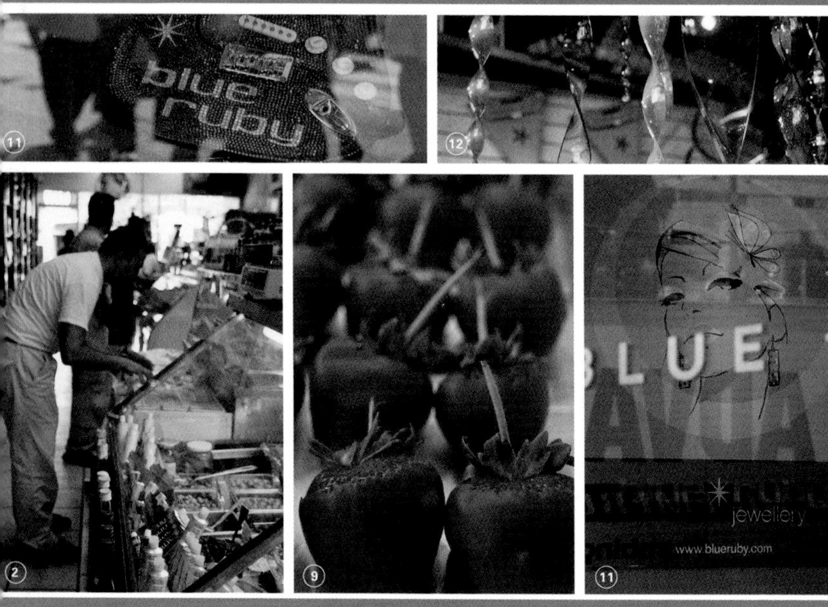
11
blue
ruby
12
2
9
BLUE
jewellery
www.blueruby.com
11

Shopping

② Swiss chocolate and Dutch licorice sell like hotcakes at the **European Delicatessen**. The name says it all - this shop sells all sorts of European specialties. Moreover, the Iranian owners make delicious sandwiches with fillings like mozzarella and smoked meat.
1220 davie street, telephone (604) 688-3442, open mon-sat 9.30am-10pm, sun 9.30am-6.30pm, bus 6 davie

⑨ Perhaps you've already noticed the window of the **Rocky Mountain Chocolate Factory**. Bars of fudge are made here right before the eyes of passing shoppers. These bars of sweetness look absolutely amazing. Besides the popular fudge, the shop also sells bonbons and ice cream.
1017 robson street, telephone (604) 688-4100, open sun-wed 9am-11pm, thu-sat 9am-midnight, bus 5 robson

⑪ Everything glimmers and shimmers in **Blue Ruby**, a store full of jewelry and accessories. In addition to lines like 'Tarina Tarantino'' you can find unique pieces from local designers here as well.
1089 robson street, telephone (604) 899-2583, open mon-thu 10am-9pm, fri 10am-10pm, sat 10am-9pm, sun 11am-8pm, bus 5 robson

⑫ This strange shop only sells holograms in different shapes and sizes. The images in them vary from Disney figures to scary wolves or a picture of a cat. Even if you don't like this sort of artistry, the **Hologram Store** is fascinating.
101-1100 robson street, telephone (604) 687-3600, open daily 10am-9pm, bus 5 robson

(13) Canadian brands such as Talula and TNA are available at **Aritzia**. There's an array of sportswear, as well as chic clothing. It can be a bit pricey, but then you'll get an item of clothing that you can only buy in Canada!
1110 robson street, telephone (604) 684-3251, open mon-tue 10am-7pm, wed-sat 10am-9pm, sun 11am-7pm, bus 5 robson

(14) Robson Street has a number of shoe stores with a surprisingly large selection of nice shoes. The sports shoes and sandals are all quite hip and reasonably priced. **Joneve** is a good place to check out.
1193 robson street, telephone (604) 602-1771, open mon-sat 10am-9pm, sun 11am-9pm, bus 5 robson

(28) **Koo-Koo** has sweet baby clothes and lovely bath towels with funny figures and animals dreamt up by a local designer. The shop is also full of soaps and other paraphernalia.
1114 denman street, telephone (604) 629-1502, open daily 11am-6pm, bus 6 davie

Joneve

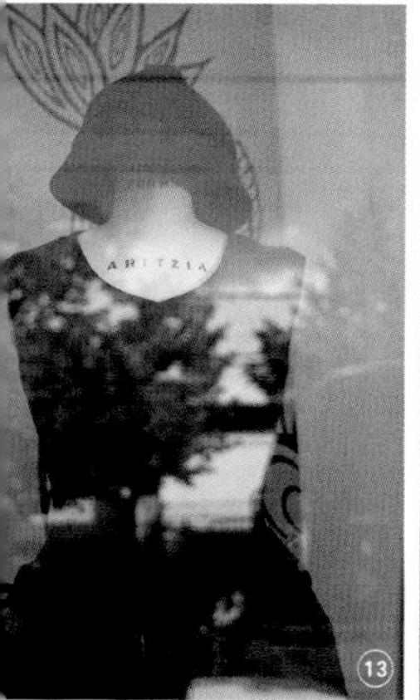

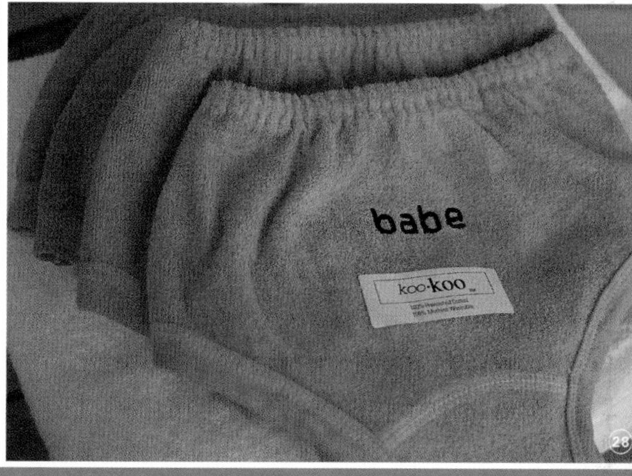

Nice to do

(18) **Harbor Cruises** are an inexpensive way to catch a beautiful view of Vancouver from the water! You can also take a cruise in English Bay and for a couple of extra dollars you can have dinner, too. The cruises last from two to four hours and you can even take a romantic evening cruise.
coal harbour, www.boatcruises.com, daily 7am-9.30pm, price per cruise $19, bus 135 stanley park

(22) At the **Vancouver Aquarium** you'll learn that jellyfish can be really beautiful and fascinating. Located in lovely Stanley Park, you can enjoy hours of fish-watching and gazing at other sea life. Favorites are the sea otters, seals and dolphins.
stanley park, telephone (604) 659-3474, www.vanaqua.org, open winter daily 10am-5.30pm, summer daily 9.30am-7pm, entrance adults $15.95, students and seniors $11.95, children from 4-12 $8.95, under 4 free, bus 135 stanley park

(23) For an active day, hire a bicycle at **Spokes Bicycle Rentals** and go for a ride in Stanley Park. This boulevard is wonderful, with breathtaking views of the ocean, Vancouver's skyline or the Lion's Gate Bridge on every corner. You can take a rest anywhere in the park and even cool off in the water park. How about a refreshing water fight in one of the different fountains?
1798 west georgia street, telephone (604) 688-5141, open daily 8am-9pm, www.vancouverbikerental.com, price bicycle $6 an hour, bus 5 robson

(29) On a hot day, you can't beat sunbathing on one of the child-friendly beaches of **English Bay**. You can choose from the busy English Bay Beach or one of the quieter Second and Third Beaches. Take a dip in the ocean to cool off - who said Canada was cold?
beach street at denman, bus 6 davie

BRITANNIA
18
22
29

West End & Downtown

WALKING TOUR 1

Take bus 6 in the direction of Davie and get off at the Jervis stop. Cross the street and follow Davie Street to the left. Enjoy some breakfast and a cup of coffee at Melriches 1 and discover the various shops and restaurants on Davie Street 2 3 4 5 6. Turn left on Hornby Street. Cross Robson Street and walk to the right for Vancouver Art Gallery 7 and visit Robson Square across the road 8. Walk back to Robson Street and turn left. You are in the shopping heart of Vancouver 9 11 12 13 14. If you're hungry after all that shopping, you can have something delicious to eat 10 or go left onto Nicola Street a bit further on. Turn right onto Barclay Street, where you will come across the Roedde House Museum on your left 15. Take the time to go for a walk in the Victorian garden before you turn right into Cardero Street. Follow this road till you reach the water, where you can go for a drink on the terrace of Cardero's 16. You are now in Coal Harbour 17, where soaring apartment and office buildings have been built in recent years. Follow the seawall to the left and stay on the path that curves along the ocean 18 19. You are walking in Stanley Park 20. Cross the street when you see the totem poles 21 and learn something about Canada's natives. Keep following the path and turn left on to the seawall. Walk along the water park and go left under the bridge for more of Stanley Park. Follow the path and on your left you'll find Vancouver Aquarium 22. At the end of the path turn right. You are now leaving Stanley Park. Head right to enter Denman Street 23 24 25 26 27 28. Cross Davie Street and walk to the English Bay Beach 29. To finish, enjoy the best view of the sunset from the roof terrace of the Boat House restaurant 30.

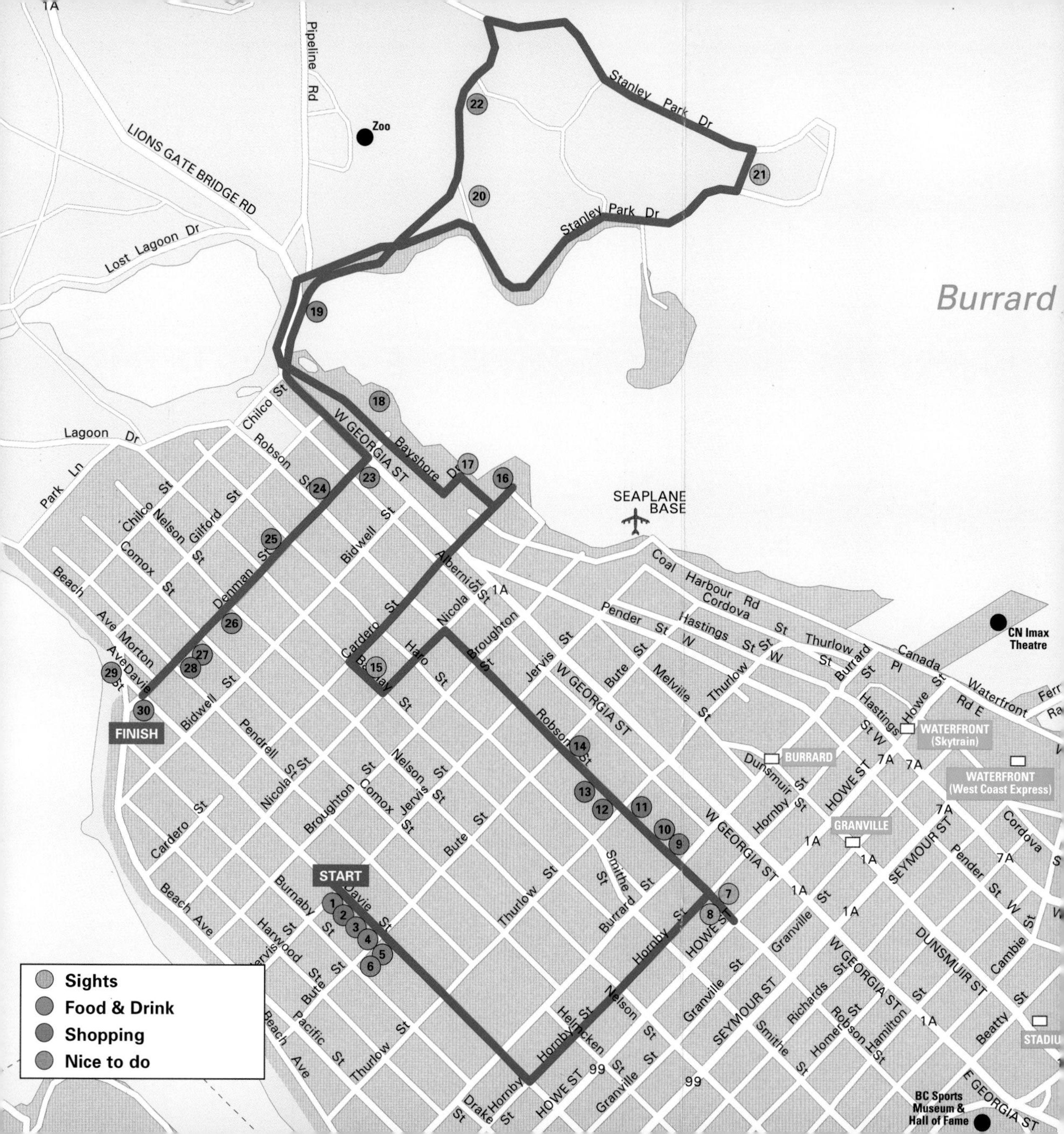

Sights
Food & Drink
Shopping
Nice to do
START
FINISH
Burrard
Zoo
Stanley Park Dr
LIONS GATE BRIDGE RD
Lost Lagoon Dr
Lagoon Dr
Pipeline Rd
Park Ln
Chilco St
Robson St
W GEORGIA ST
Bayshore Dr
SEAPLANE BASE
Coal Harbour Rd
Cordova St
Pender St
Hastings St W
Thurlow St
Burrard St
Canada Pl
Waterfront Rd E
CN Imax Theatre
WATERFRONT (Skytrain)
WATERFRONT (West Coast Express)
BURRARD
GRANVILLE
STADIUM
BC Sports Museum & Hall of Fame
E GEORGIA ST
Denman St
Gilford St
Nelson St
Comox St
Bidwell St
Alberni St
Nicola St
Cardero St
Barclay St
Haro St
Broughton St
Jervis St
Bute St
Melville St
Dunsmuir St
Hornby St
HOWE ST
SEYMOUR ST
Granville St
Richards St
Homer St
Hamilton St
Robson St
Cambie St
Beatty St
Smithe St
Helmcken St
Drake St
Pacific St
Harwood St
Burnaby St
Davie St
Pendrell St
Morton Ave
Beach Ave
DUNSMUIR ST
1A
7A
99

1 Melriches
2 European Delicatessen
3 Ho Ho Fast Food
4 Stepho's
5 Hamburger Mary's
6 Jupiter Café
7 Vancouver Art Gallery
8 Robson Square
9 Rocky Mountain Chocolate Factory
10 Tsunami Sushi
11 Blue Ruby
12 Hologram Store
13 Aritzia
14 Joneve
15 Roedde House Museum
16 Cardero's
17 Coal Harbour
18 Harbour Cruises
19 Vancouver Rowing Club
20 Stanley Park
21 Totem Poles
22 Vancouver Aquarium
23 Spokes Bicycle Rentals
24 Mum's Gelati
25 Ukrainian Village
26 Brass Monkey
27 Banana Leaf
28 Koo-Koo
29 English Bay
30 Boat House Restaurant

- **Sights**
- **Food & Drink**
- **Shopping**
- **Nice to do**

Gastown & Chinatown

Gastown is Vancouver's oldest neighborhood and has been through some turbulent times in its history. It suffered a huge fire in 1886 and later, from the 1940s to the 1960s, was an extremely impoverished part of town.
In the 1970s, Gastown was given the status of a historical monument by the governing bodies of the province. The well-preserved architecture and narrow brick roads give the area a European feeling. Now full of souvenir shops and restaurants, Gastown is the main tourist attraction of Vancouver.

2

Fascinating Chinatown begins a few streets further on. It is almost like you've landed in China as you navigate the busy shopping streets, which smell like soap, fish and tea and where almost everyone speaks Chinese (nearly 35,000 Asians live in this area). Go shopping here for authentic Chinese ingredients you can use to create a delicious meal or just wander around, taking in the atmosphere and enjoying yummy, exotic food. Unfortunately, in order to get to Chinatown from Gastown you have to go through a couple of shady streets where drugs and crime are prevalent. During the day it is safe, but take care that you don't walk alone at night.

6x zeker doen!

Seaplanes

Watch seaplanes take off from the boulevard

Steam Clock

Get your photo taken

Dr. Sun Yat-Sen Garden

Take a fascinating tour

Ten Ren's Tea & Ginseng

Browse and buy Chinese tea

Golden Town Book Store

Drink bubble tea

Chinatown's Night Market

Visit this Chinatown landmark

- **Sights**
- **Shopping**
- **Food & Drink**
- **Nice to do**

STEAM CLOCK ⑩

Sights

(1) The Canadian Pacific Railway Express used to be one of Canada's most well known companies. The train was an important means of transport in the early 1900s and in 1912, a prestigious station was built in honor of the Pacific Railway. This is now known as **Waterfront Station**, and even though the Pacific Railway Express no longer exists, the stately station building is still used as a station for the skytrain and seabus.
601 west cordova, telephone (604) 488-8906, not open to the public, skytrain waterfront

(2) The World Trade Center in Vancouver, **Canada Place**, was inherited from the 1986 World Fair. It is now a port for cruise ships and has a conference center and many hotels. Enjoy a beautiful view of the ocean from here.
canada place, 999 canada place way, telephone (604) 681-2111, not open to the public, bus 135 stanley park

(7) **Hudson House** was once used as a trading center for fur and alcohol. It was also very important for gold diggers during the Gold Rush, who bought their groceries here. It now houses a souvenir shop, and it is striking how much of the original architecture the owner has tried to preserve.
321 water street, telephone (604) 687-4781, www.hudsonhousetrading.com, open daily 9am-6pm, skytrain waterfront

(10) Gastown is famous for a somewhat strange attraction. The **Steam Clock** is a replica from 1875; the mechanism works completely on steam and blows its whistle every 15 minutes.
corner of water street and cambie street, skytrain waterfront

(13) Visit the picturesque **Mews Courtyard** if you need to take a rest from the hustle and bustle of the city. It is difficult to imagine that this was the location of Vancouver's first prison.
12 water street, skytrain waterfront

13
22
1

2
15

16 GASSY JACK

⑮ After the huge fire of 1886, the **Europe Hotel** was the first hotel to be made from concrete instead of wood. An Italian businessman constructed this beautiful building in 1908. At that time it was the best hotel in the city. It hasn't been a hotel for ages, however, and now houses a lovely interior shop on the ground floor with apartments on the floors above.
43 powell street, upper floors not open to the public, skytrain waterfront

⑯ The name 'Gastown' comes from Jack Leighton, the owner of a popular saloon. The story goes that he was an unbelievable 'fast talker' which earned him the nickname **Gassy Jack**. A sculpture of him can be admired on the Old Maple Tree Square where, in 1885, pioneers chose the name Vancouver for their new city.
corner of carrall street and alexander street, skytrain waterfront

⑱ The corner of East Pender Street is the location for an extremely narrow house with a rich history. In 1912, the government wanted to widen the street and the owner of the property, Chang Toy, had to turn the land in. Later, he received a small portion of it back. Toy couldn't leave it alone and built a very narrow house on that small piece of land. This is now called the **Sam Kee Building**.
8 east pender street, not open to the public, skytrain stadium

⑲ You wouldn't know it when you see the newly built apartments, but **Shanghai Alley** is the oldest street in Chinatown. This street marked the beginning of Chinatown in 1885.
between carrall street and taylor street, skytrain stadium

㉒ The best place to find out more about China and Chinese Vancouver is at the **Chinese Cultural Center and Museum & Archives**. You can visit exhibits about the generations of Chinese families that have come to Vancouver. The Chinese-Canadian Military Museum can also be found on the second floor.
555 columbia street, telephone (604) 658-8880, www.cccvan.com,
open tue-sun 11am-5pm, entrance adults $4, students $3, skytrain stadium

Food & Drink

⑤ At **Steamworks**, have a taste of freshly brewed beers. This is also a good place for delicious food. There is a special ambiance downstairs in the cellar that you can't find anywhere else in Vancouver.
375 water street, telephone (604) 689-2739, open daily 11.30am-midnight, price $14, skytrain waterfront

⑥ Go down a small staircase to find a truly authentic Italian atmosphere at **Il Giardino di Umberto Ristorante**. The plastered walls are painted in either soft yellow or terracotta colors and the food here is outstanding. Watch out when the bill comes, however... you'll have to dig deep into your pockets.
1382 hornby street, telephone (604) 669-2422, open mon-fri 11.30am-11pm, sat 5.30pm-11pm, price $25, skytrain waterfront

⑨ The **Water Street Café** is located on a lovely corner of Gastown. Thanks to the large terrace, it's a very popular café for drinks in the summer. You can eat delicious 'west coast' style food here, like wonderful salmon dishes, pasta or steak.
300 water street, telephone (604) 879-2832, open daily 11.30am-midnight, price $15, skytrain waterfront

⑭ If you often avoid Thai food because you find it to be too spicy, try **Thai Palace**. They serve delicious authentic Thai dishes and you can tell them exactly how you would like to have it prepared - mild, medium or spicy.
100 water street, telephone (604) 331-1660, open daily 11.30am-10pm, price $14, skytrain waterfront

⑰ Visit the **Irish Heather** for coziness and the specialties of an authentic Irish Pub. Go all the way to the back for the best spot in the café and enjoy the live music played by the group of musicians sitting at the table next to you - of course don't forget to order a pint of Guinness.
217 carrall street, telephone (604) 688-9779, open daily noon-midnight, price $15, skytrain waterfront station

WATERSTREET CAFE ⑨

OO'S HO HO
ESTAURANT
33
28
30
STEAMWORKS
PUB · BREWERY
5

(28) Want to be sure you eat well tonight? Then be sure to go to **Hon's Wun Tun House**. It is difficult to choose between all of the delicious dishes. Discover the difference between 'potstickers', 'gyozas' and 'dim sum'! Keep in mind that you can only pay cash here.
108-268 keefer street, telephone (604) 688-0871, open daily 8.30am-10pm, price $7, skytrain stadium

(30) Try the Chinese barbecue for a traditional lunch at the **Garden Restaurant**. The atmosphere of Chinatown follows you inside, so you can enjoy it during your meal as well. Only open for breakfast and lunch.
249 east pender, telephone (604) 682-1608, open daily 7.30am-6pm, price $7, dim sum $2, skytrain stadium

(33) **Foo's Ho Ho Restaurant** is fantastic! Come prepared for delicious, traditional, Chinese cuisine that probably tastes very different to the Chinese take-out you're used to. Stimulate your taste buds by trying things you've never even heard of.
102 east pender, telephone (604) 609-2889, open mon-sat 11am-10pm, sun 4pm-10pm, price $12, skytrain stadium

Shopping

⑧ You can buy the best souvenirs at **Michelle's**, which sells practically every kind of souvenir to be had in Vancouver: from t-shirts to reindeer fleece, and from postcards to sheep's wool sweaters. Take the time to compare prices, because sometimes you can buy the same souvenirs cheaper elsewhere.
73 water street, telephone (604) 687-5930, open daily 9am-9pm, skytrain waterfront

(11) At **Hill's Native Art** you can buy art by Canadian artists. A large selection of it is 'native art', made according to the traditions of native Canadians. Some of the pieces are definitely worth seeing. Take a look at the gallery on the first floor, too.
165 water street, telephone (604) 682-4427, open daily 9am-9pm, skytrain waterfront

(12) If you love tobacco and cigars, you should definitely visit the **Cigar Connoisseur**. The friendly owner helps you make a choice and explains the differences between the different cigars. Then, sit back in a roomy chair to smoke your cigar and look around at the cases where the cigars are displayed.
101-12 water street, telephone (604) 682-4427, open daily 10am-9pm, skytrain waterfront

(23) The aroma of tea greets you at the door of **Ten Ren's Tea & Ginseng**. You can get fantastic Chinese tea here, from very strong leaves to milder green tea. Ginseng, which is a remedy for all sorts of ailments, is sold here in all shapes and sizes. Chinese people use it against old age symptoms and for building up resistance. Some types of ginseng are very rare and expensive. Don't forget to ask about side effects and instructions for use.
550 main street, telephone (604) 689-7598, open daily 9.30am-6pm, skytrain stadium

(24) According to Chinese tradition, jade is a lucky stone. In Chinatown, you won't see very many ladies who don't wear jade jewelry. At **Lucky Jade Jewelry** you can find lots of different types of jade. Test if it is real by rubbing it on your clothes a couple of times. If the stone still feels cold when you put it to your cheek, then it's the real thing!
210 keefer street, telephone (604) 689-8810, open mon-fri 11am-6pm, skytrain stadium

(25) There are many supermarkets in Chinatown, but one the most unique is the **Chinatown Supermarket**. This is a huge shop where you'll find aquariums with live crabs, lobsters and other seafood in the back of the store. You'll even be surprised by the assortment available in the meat department.
239 keefer street, telephone (604) 685-3583, open mon-sat 8.30am-6.30pm, skytrain stadium

(26) The remedies and drinks you can get at **Cheng Fung Herbs** probably all work, but unfortunately all the labels are in Chinese and you probably won't have a clue what they are. In any case they are very decorative and fascinating. Let yourself be surprised by how many different herbs one store can carry.
245 keefer street, telephone (604) 331-0992, open daily 8am-9pm, skytrain stadium

(27) To get a good assortment of Chinese cakes and pastries, go to **Maxim's Bakery**. This bake shop has been open for at least 25 years and makes wonderful mango cakes and lemon pastries. The coconut rolls and Chinese donuts are also very delicious.
257 keefer street, telephone (604) 688-6281, open daily 8am-6pm, skytrain stadium

(31) **Bamboo City** is a good place for Chinatown souvenirs. It is difficult to choose between the colorful lanterns, cushions and fans. At the back of the shop you can admire Chinese antiques and porcelain.
135 east pender street, telephone (604) 662-3300, open daily 9.30am-6pm, skytrain stadium

(32) A Chinese specialty that you really should try is 'Bubble tea'. At the **Golden Crown Bookstore** you can get this milkshake-type tea in all kinds of flavors. The bubbles are made from chewy tapioca. At the back of the store you'll find Chinese language books, which are interesting to leaf through. The Chinese comic books are especially entertaining!
138 east pender street, telephone (604) 688-2281, open daily 10am-6pm, skytrain stadium

Nice to do

(3) Walking around Canada Place you'll suddenly come across a harbor for seaplanes. **Harbour Air** provides flights to and from Vancouver Island or other small islands in the area. It is a fast way to travel, but definitely not cheap. Luckily it's also interesting to watch how the planes take off and land.
canada place, telephone (604) 274-1277, www.harbour-air.com, price for a scenic tour $89, skytrain waterfront

(4) Vancouver is an impressive city when seen from the **Harbour Center Look Out**. An elevator takes you to the highest point in 50 seconds where you'll have a fantastic view of the whole city. While having a bite to eat at the restaurant, take your time to look around and enjoy the view. Don't rush - your ticket is valid all day. If you go during the day, you can come back at night for the 'Vancouver by night' experience.
555 west hastings street, telephone (604) 669-2220, www.vancouverlookout.com, open winter daily 9am-9pm, summer daily 8.30am-10.30pm, bus 135 stanley park

(20) For a spiritually enriching experience, take a tour in the **Dr. Sun Yat-Sen Garden**. This garden was built according to the traditions of the Ming dynasty. There are references all over the garden to Buddhism, Taoism and the ideas of Yin and Yang. This is a hidden treasure in Vancouver!
578 carrall street, telephone (604) 662-3207, www.vancouverchinesegarden.com, open summer daily 10am-6pm, winter daily 10am-4.30pm, entrance adult $8.25, students $5.75, skytrain stadium

(21) Right next to the garden, you'll find the **Dr. Sun Yat-Sen Park**. In this park, just like the gardens, aspects of Chinese traditions are prevalent. For example, the water is not cloudy because it is dirty but because this way the green color of the lucky jade stones glitter in the sunshine. The park is a wonderful place to get away from the frantic pace of Chinatown.
578 carrall street, entrance free, skytrain stadium

29 From June to September, there is a **Night Market** in Chinatown every Friday, Saturday and Sunday, completely decorated with lamps and lighting. This is when Chinatown is at its liveliest. You can either wander through the stands or do some serious shopping for the evening meal.
200 blocks from keefer street, open june to september fri-sun 6.30pm-11.30pm, skytrain stadium

Chinatown & Gastown

WALKING TOUR 2

Take the skytrain to Waterfront Station (1). Walk out of the station and go right on to Cordova Street. Go right on Howe Street so you are walking towards Canada Place (2). Walk up the stairs on the right-hand side of the building. You can walk around the entire building for a view of the ocean (3). Leaving Canada Place behind you, cross the street and walk through the park with the waterfalls. Cross the street here and go to the stairs on the left of West Hastings Street (4). Turn left on to Richards Street. Cross Cordova Street and go to the right onto Water Street. This is where the heart of Gastown begins, with numerous historical buildings, restaurants and shops (5) (6) (7) (8) (9) (10) (11) (12) (13) (14) (15) (16). Keep following Water Street until you get to Carrall Street. After having a drink at Irish Heather (17), turn right on Carrall Street. Unfortunately, you now have to go through two streets where there is a lot of drug-related crime. It is not advisable to walk around here alone at night, but during the day it is no problem. If you'd rather not walk, take bus 210 here and get off at Pender Street or take a taxi. Go right into Pender Street to see the Sam Kee Building (18) and the Chinese port, built in honor of the last millennium. Afterwards go into the Shanghai Alley (19), where you can read about the history of Chinatown on the monument at the end of the alley. Cross Carrall Street to get to the Dr. Sun Yat-Sen Garden (20) with the Dr. Sun Yat-Sen Park (21) behind it. Walk through the park and at the exit you'll find the Chinese Cultural Center on your left (22). Cross Columbia Street and turn into Keefer Street. You will now feel as though you are in China, with wonderful shops and markets (23) (24) (25) (26) (27) (28) (29). Go left on Gore Street and then go directly left again on East Pender Street (30) (31) (32) (33). Walk out of Chinatown and go right on Columbia Street. Again go through the shady streets and then on to the old railway. Turn left into Gastown, where you will find nice places to have a drink in a bar or outside on a terrace in the sun.

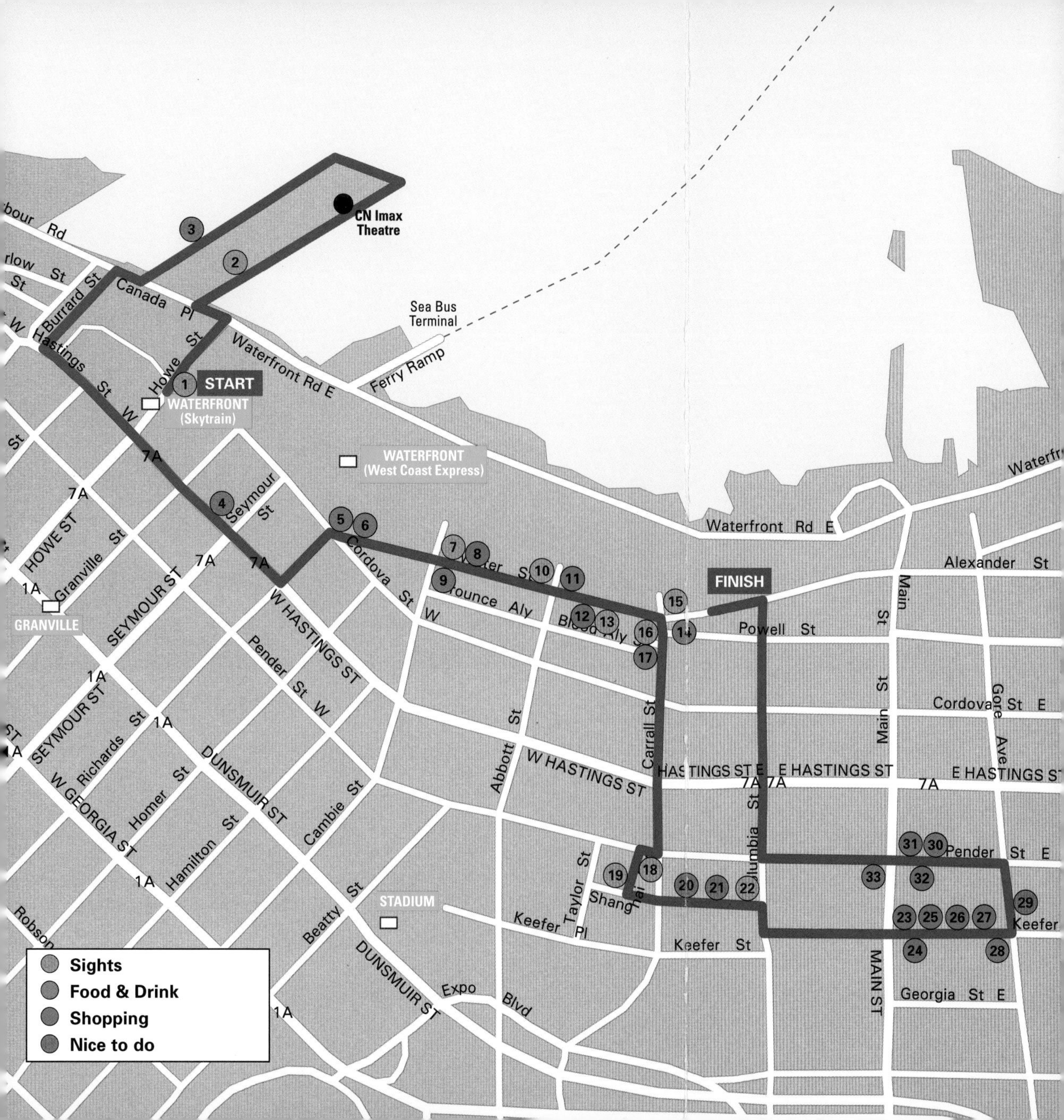
CN Imax Theatre
Sea Bus Terminal
START
FINISH
WATERFRONT (Skytrain)
WATERFRONT (West Coast Express)
GRANVILLE
STADIUM
Canada Pl
Howe St
Waterfront Rd E
Ferry Ramp
Burrard St
W Hastings St
Seymour St
Cordova St W
Water St
Trounce Aly
Blood Aly
Powell St
Alexander St
Main St
Cordova St E
Gore Ave
W HASTINGS ST
E HASTINGS ST
Pender St W
Pender St E
Carrall St
Columbia St
Abbott St
Taylor St
Shanghai
Keefer Pl
Keefer St
Georgia St E
MAIN ST
DUNSMUIR ST
W GEORGIA ST
HOWE ST
SEYMOUR ST
Granville St
Richards St
Homer St
Hamilton St
Cambie St
Beatty St
Expo Blvd
Robson
Sights
Food & Drink
Shopping
Nice to do

1. Waterfront Station
2. Canada Place
3. Harbour Air
4. Harbour Center Look Out
5. Steamworks
6. Il Giardino di Umberto Ristorante
7. Hudson House
8. Michelle's
9. Waterstreet Café
10. Steam Clock
11. Hill's Native Art
12. Cigar Connaisseur
13. Mews Courtyard
14. Thai Palace
15. Europe Hotel
16. Gassy Jack
17. Irish Heather
18. Sam Kee Building
19. Shanghai Alley
20. Dr. Sun Yat-Sen Garden
21. Dr. Sun Yat-Sen Park
22. Chinese Cultural Center
23. Ten Ren's Tea & Ginseng
24. Lucky Jade Jewelry
25. Chinatown Supermarket
26. Cheng Fung Herbs
27. Maxim's Bakery
28. Hon's Wun Tun House
29. Night market
30. Garden Restaurant
31. Bamboo City
32. Golden Crown Bookstore
33. Foo's Ho Ho Restaurant

- **Sights**
- **Food & Drink**
- **Shopping**
- **Nice to do**

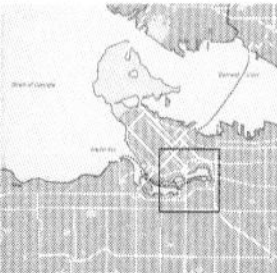

Yaletown

If you're young and rich in Vancouver, chances are you live in Yaletown. This is the area where the city's yuppies hang out and, as a consequence, has become very expensive. You'll find a number of chic restaurants and exclusive boutiques in this part of town, which is often compared to SoHo in New York and London.

The transformation of Yaletown began in the 1980s and 90s, when old warehouses that were being used as parking garages began to be renovated into hip restaurants, trendy boutiques and exclusive beauty salons. These days, the heart of Yaletown swells with soaring, luxury apartment buildings filled with the upwardly mobile.

3

The best way to get to know the area is to window-shop in the lovely but pricey stores. On the way, you'll pass stylish residents relaxing on terraces of fine restaurants and enjoying a fantastic meal with a glass of expensive wine. You'll certainly find the best service in Yaletown, but remember everything comes at a price.

When you've had enough of shopping and looking around, get some fresh air on the beautiful nearby boulevard.

6 Musts!

Boulevard

Begin the day begins with a nice walk

GM Place stadion

Catch the action of Canada's favorite sport

Urban Fare

Buy what you need for your evening meal

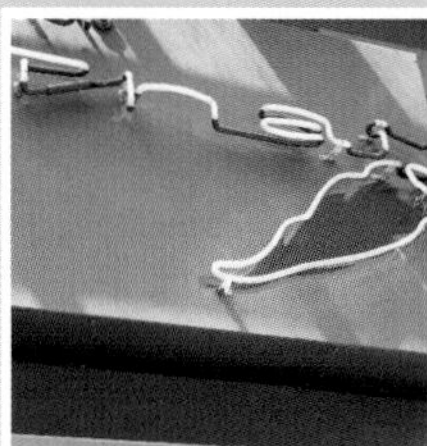

Simply Thai

Order the cho muang

Global Atomic Design

Try on the newest Adidas

Blue Water Café

One of many chic restaurants

- Sights
- Shopping
- Food & Drink
- Nice to do

SCIENCE WORLD ①

Sights

① **Science World** is a dome-shaped metal building that shimmers in the sunlight. You'll learn all sorts of things about science in this museum, which is especially fun for children, since you can touch everything and most exhibits are interactive. Come up with your own invention or enjoy a film on a huge, three-dimensional screen in the OMNIMAX, located on the third floor.
1455 quebec street, telephone (604) 443-7443, www.scienceworld.bc.ca, open mon-fri 10am-5pm, sun 10am-6pm, entrance adults $12.75, students and children up to 18 $8.50, skytrain science world

② The **Plaza of Nations** was built for the 1986 World's Fair. It now houses a couple of restaurants with an excellent view of the boulevard and has rooms available for big parties and events. It is an impressive building with lots of glass, and has a plaza where skateboarders show off their stunts.
b100-750 pacific boulevard, telephone (604) 682-0777, www.plazaofnations.com, not open to the public, skytrain stadium

⑤ One of the nicest neighborhood community centers in Vancouver is the **Roundhouse Community Center**. Walk-ins are welcome and you never know what interesting exhibit you might come across. Dance and theater performances are held here occasionally and the Roundhouse Center is also a central point during Vancouver's jazz festival.
181 roundhouse mews, telephone (604) 713-1800, www.roundhouse.ca, performance $5, skytrain stadium

⑰ The **public library** in Vancouver is a modern version of the Coliseum in Rome and is stunning! You'll find a number of restaurants in the covered gallery on the ground floor and Library Square in front is a wonderful place to have a sandwich on a warm afternoon.
350 west georgia street, telephone (604) 331-3600, www.vpl.ca, free entrance, open mon-thu 10am-8pm, fri-sat 10am-5pm, sun 1pm-5pm, bus 15 cambie

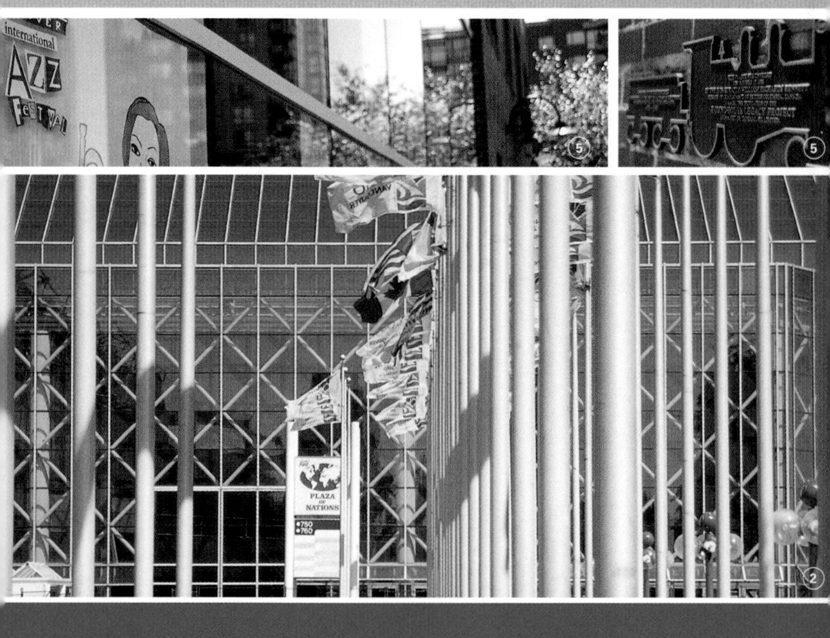
international
FESTIVAL
PLAZA
OF
NATIONS
5
5
2

10
10
10
LICENSED
6
OYSTERS
LOBSTER
CRAB
PRAWN
SEA FOOD PARLOR
FOR
LADIES AND GENTLEMEN
CLAMS
MUSSELS
QUAHOGS
OYSTERS
9

Food & Drink

⑥ There is a real French atmosphere at **Café O**, where you can order a delicious cup of coffee and a French baguette and read the paper in a corner. Make sure you sit at the window so that in between sips of your coffee you can watch all the hip Yaletowners walking by.
302 davie street, telephone (604) 694-2240, open mon-fri 7am-6pm, sat-sun 8am-6pm, price coffee $2, skytrain science world

⑦ Pull up a chair for a delicious French meal at **Elixir**. This is a real French bistro, serving breakfast, lunch and dinner. It's actually a part of the Opus hotel, but non-hotel guests are also welcome.
350 davie street, telephone (604) 642-0557, open mon-sat 6.30am-2am, sun 6.30am-midnight, price $25, skytrain stadium

⑨ If you love fish, you'll definitely enjoy a meal at **Rodney's Oyster House**. The interior makes the food even tastier, with tables made of white wood and an authentic beach house feeling. The wonderful fish aroma greets you upon entering and the bar is very inviting, too. Try the 'chowder' or 'steamer' made with the fish of your choice.
1228 hamilton street, telephone (604) 609-0080, open daily 11.30am-midnight, price $20, skytrain stadium

⑩ At **Simply Thai**, the chef is from Thailand and was trained by the Thai Royal cook! Try the 'cho muang" served in a flower handmade out of dough. If you plan to eat here, be sure to make reservations - especially on the weekend.
1211 hamilton street, telephone (604) 642-0123, open mon-fri 11.30am-3pm, 5pm-11pm, sat 5pm-11pm, sun 5pm-10pm, price $13, skytrain stadium

16 SUBEEZ CAFE

⑬ **Cioppino's Enoteca** is a super-deluxe Italian restaurant serving heavenly Mediterranean food. Enjoy small decadent snacks on the wonderful terrace.
1129-1133 hamilton street, telephone (604) 685-8462, open mon-sat noon-3pm, 5.30pm-11pm, price $24, skytrain stadium

⑮ The **Blue Water Café** opened its doors two years ago and fits perfectly into Yaletown. The menu consists mainly of delicious fish dishes such as sushi. In addition to a magnificent terrace, the interior is lovely, with lots of dark brown wood contrasting with the marine-blue glasses shown off on every table.
1095 hamilton street, telephone (604) 688-8078, open daily 11.30am-midnight, price $30, skytrain stadium

⑯ On the edge of Yaletown, you'll find **Subeez Café**, a huge bar decorated in industrial style. The art on the cement walls is often very daring and is replaced every three months. The food is good and inexpensive and, aside from beer and wine, you can order delicious tea.
891 homer street, telephone (604) 687-6143, open mon-fri 11.30am-1am, sat 11am-1am, sun 11am-midnight, price $14, bus 15 cambie

⑱ Eating real Spanish tapas at **El Patio** is a lot of fun. This restaurant is hidden away, but that's what makes it extra special. Order a few tapas and a jug of sangria and you're good to go - and it won't even cost a fortune!
891 cambie street, telephone (604) 681-9149, open mon-sat 5pm-midnight, price $12, bus 15 cambie

(22) **Section 3** fits right in on this street. The first thing you notice upon entering is the interior - lots of color, austere, modern tables and chairs and hip waitresses. You can have dinner or just grab a drink and really soak in the character of Yaletown. The area's yuppies love being seen lounging on the terrace or spending money at the bar.
1039 mainland street, telephone (604) 684-2777, open mon-wed 11.30am-midnight, thu 11.30am-1am, fri-sat 11.30am-2am, sun 5pm-midnight, price $20, skytrain stadium

(26) **Boulangerie la Parisienne** is a great place to rest up after a long day of sightseeing and is an ideal place for a delicious, authentic croissant or other French pastries.
1076 mainland street, telephone (604) 682-2176, open mon-fri 7am-7pm, sat 8am-7pm, 9am-5pm, price coffee $1.75, skytrain stadium

(28) Discover the fun of eating your meals on skewers at **Glowbal Grill & Satay Bar**. While you enjoy the minimalist, modern interior, the waiting staff will help you make a choice from the extensive menu. After dinner you can 'lounge' in the Afterglow - the room at the back of the restaurant with couches, a bar and a DJ. This is a fun place to stop by for a drink as well.
1079 mainland street, telephone (604) 602-0835, open mon-fri 11.30am-1am, sat-sun 10.30am-1am, $20, skytrain stadium

(29) **Yaletown Brewing Co.** is an enormous restaurant with its own brewery serving freshly brewed beer like the 'Mainland Lager.' You can have a delicious lunch or dinner, and when you've had enough to eat, request a tour of the small brewery.
1111 mainland street, telephone (604) 681-2739, open sun-wed 11.30am-midnight, thu-sat 11.30am-1am, price $16, skytrain stadium

eat.
drink.
22

11
roo
homew
8
8

Shopping

(4) Even the supermarket in Yaletown is trendy and upscale. It's great fun to shop at **Urban Fare**, with its predominately fresh food selection. Sometimes, however, the definition of the word 'fresh' gets carried a bit far. How would you like to pay $100 for bread that was just flown in from Paris?
177 davie street, telephone (604) 975-7550, open daily 6am-midnight, skytrain stadium

(8) Two Australian artists make jewelry, dishes and cups from surfboards and two traveling sisters sell them in Vancouver. **Roost** is a truly unique place and one place to find everything from the Dinosaur Designs label - and a lot more.
1192 hamilton street, telephone (604) 708-0084, open mon-sat 10am-6pm, sun noon-5pm, skytrain stadium

(11) **Curious** is one of those shops where you can always find something you like. It's a good place for gifts, knick-knacks and cute underwear.
1150 hamilton street, telephone (604) 488-1151, open mon-sat 10am-6pm, sun 11am-5pm, skytrain stadium

(12) At **Zero Gravity** you can find men's and women's Italian clothing brands. In addition to labels like Energie and Miss Sixty, there are quite a few lesser-known labels that are definitely worth checking out. Be warned... you might be spending a lot of time in the dressing room.
1042 hamilton street, telephone (604) 688-0828, open mon-thu 11am-6pm, sat 11am-5.30pm, sun 1pm-5pm, skytrain stadium

(14) Are you looking for that cream you've seen in all the expensive magazines? You're sure to find it at **Beauty Mark**. Browse through the best brands for hair, skin and face care. Fresh, for example, is one luxury brand they carry and Deserving Thyme (a local brand) is quite reasonably priced.
1120 hamilton street, telephone (604) 642-2294, open mon-sat 10am-7pm, sun noon-5pm, skytrain stadium

⑨ The newest fashions from G-sus and Adidas can be discovered at **Global Atomic Designs Inc**. Check out the counter as well, which is full of flyers advertising parties featuring the hippest DJs.
1006 mainland street, telephone (604) 806-6223, open mon-sun 11.30am-7pm, thu-fri 11.30am-9pm, skytrain stadium

⑳ At **Fine Finds** you're sure to discover something to suit every home - check out the tablecloths with cute motifs, tableware in fun colors and bed linen made from beautiful fabrics.
1014 mainland street, telephone (604) 669-8325, open mon-sat 10am-6pm, sun 1pm-5pm, skytrain stadium

㉑ In Yaletown you can get brands that you can't find anywhere else in the city. **Tenthirtyeight clothing** is a great place to get the newest items from Stüssy. The hats are particularly popular.
1035 mainland street, telephone (604) 669-6469, open mon-sat 10am-6pm, sun 2pm-5pm, skytrain stadium

㉓ The dressing rooms at **Atomic Model** are like a fairytale - pink and pastel colored curtains hang like mosquito nets. In addition to clothes, this store also sells perfumes that correspond to your star sign.
1036 mainland street, telephone (604) 688-9989, open mon-sat 11am-7pm, sun noon-6pm, skytrain stadium

㉕ For trendy shoes like the newest Pumas or Diesels try **Intra Venus Shoes**, a tiny shoe shop with a really nice collection.
1072 mainland street, telephone (604) 685-9696, open mon-thu 11.30am-6pm, fri 11.30am-7pm, sat 11.30am-6pm, sun 1pm-5pm, skytrain stadium

㉗ After having tasted all kinds of delicious food in the restaurants of Yaletown, you can become even more inspired at **Barbara-Jo's Books to Cooks**. This store only carries cookbooks, and often hosts cooking demonstrations given by cooks and cookbook authors. If you've got time, this is an interesting way to spend an evening.
1128 mainland street, telephone (604) 688-6755, open mon-sat 10am-6pm, sun 11am-5pm, skytrain stadium

㉚ For inexpensive jeans, check out **Mavi Jeans** - great styles for under 100 dollars!
1081 mainland street, telephone (604) 669-2373, open sun-wed 10am-6pm, thu-sat 10am-8pm, skytrain stadium

BAMBU
the salon

Nice to do

③ Canada's most popular sport is ice hockey and the local team is the Vancouver Canucks (a friendly nickname for Canadians). Go see a game at **GM Place** and help get the team going by joining the crowd in a cheer of 'Go Canucks Go!'
800 griffiths way, telephone (604) 899-7400, www.canucks.com, entrance $30-$100, skytrain stadium

㉔ Yaletown wouldn't be Yaletown without a number of ritzy beauty salons and **Bambu** is one of the best. Come here for a new hairstyle or, if you like, a new hair color. By the way, that thing you used to know as a perm is now called 'hair-forming' and is one of the many choices you'll have here. The price of your new look depends on the experience and skill of your hairstylist.
1141 mainland street, telephone (604) 488-8873, www.bambuthesalon.com, open mon-wed 10am-6pm, thu-fri 10am-9pm, sat 10am-7pm, price hair cut $60, skytrain stadium

Yaletown

WALKING TOUR 3

Get off the skytrain at the Science World stop and walk out of the right side of the station. Cross Quebec Street in the direction of the Science World Museum (1). Walk up the left side of the boulevard and follow the water. Keep left at the parking lot of Plaza of Nations (2) and the Vancouver Canucks (3) stadium (GM Place). Cross the square diagonally to the right and follow the boulevard to the right. Walk past the traffic circle and cross Marina Crescent. You can do some shopping here (4) or see an exhibit (5). Keep following Davie Street and cross Pacific Boulevard. Enjoy a delicious cup of coffee at Café O (6) or Elixir (7) and browse around at Roost (8). Turn left on Hamilton Street for Rodney's Oyster Bar (9) and Simply Thai (10). Backtrack and cross Davie Street, then keep following Hamilton Street. You'll easily see how these expensive shops and restaurants (11) (12) (13) (14) (15) used to be warehouses. What used to be storage spaces are now lovely terraces. Cross Helmcken Street for a drink at Subeez (16). Go left on Homer Street and take in the beauty of Library Square (17). After you've had a rest on the stairs of the library turn left on Robson Street, then right on Cambie (18) and right again at Nelson Street. If you go left at Mainland Street, you'll find yourself in the heart of Yaletown and can do some shopping at, for example, Global Anatomic Designs Inc. (19) or Fine Finds (20). You'll definitely find a shop you like (21) (23) (25) (27) and if you're hungry or thirsty from all of that shopping you've got a huge choice of nice restaurants and cafés (22) (26). Or go for a new look to go with your new outfits (24). If you want to eat like a Yaletowner, go to Glowbal (28) and try the satay bar! If you prefer to have a beer at the local brewery, visit the Yaletown Brewing Co. (29). Afterwards walk to Mavi (30) for a cheap pair of jeans.

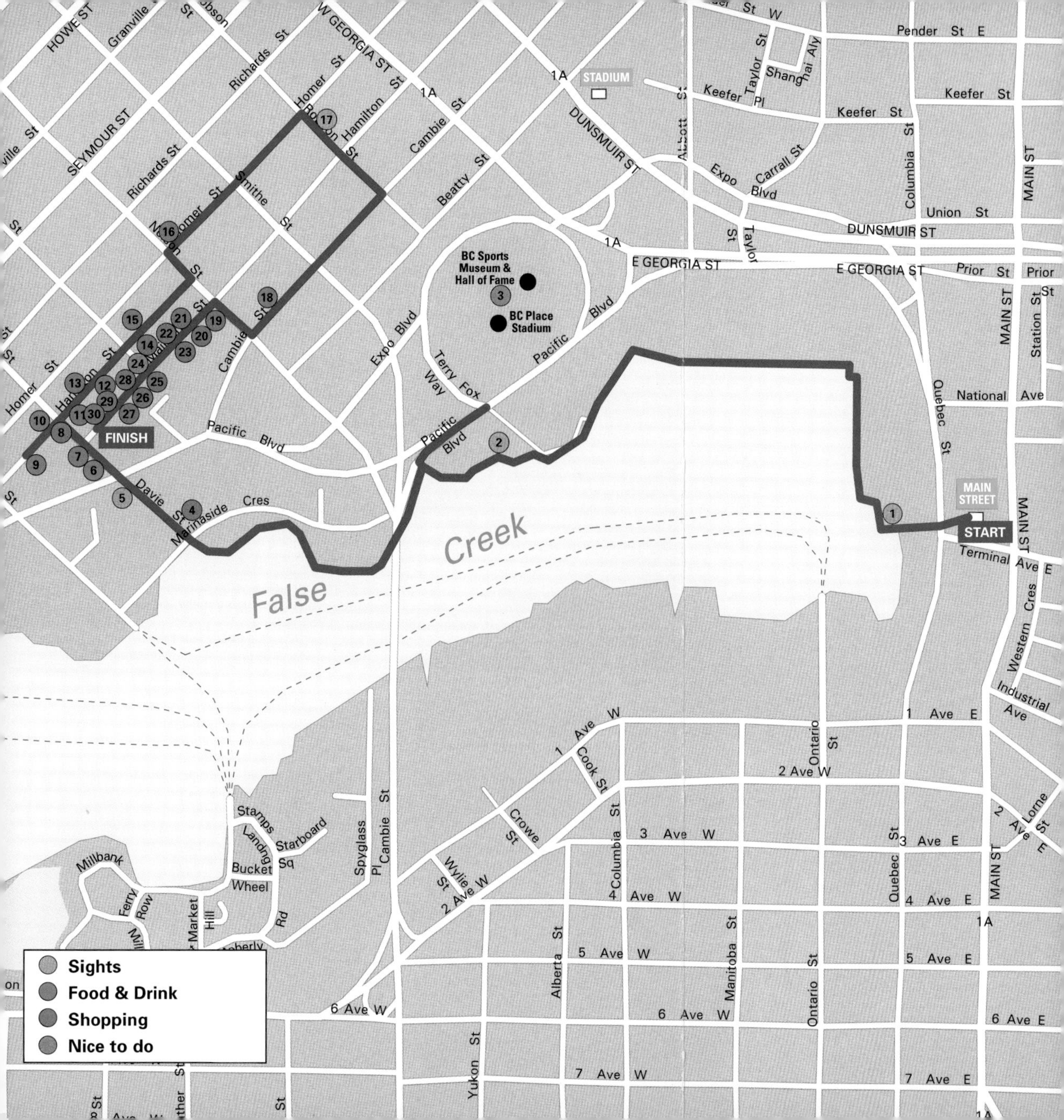

START
FINISH
MAIN STREET
STADIUM
BC Sports Museum & Hall of Fame
BC Place Stadium
False Creek
Sights
Food & Drink
Shopping
Nice to do

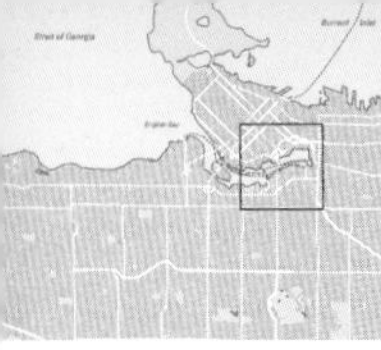

1. Science World
2. Plaza of Nations
3. GM Place
4. Urban Fare
5. Roundhouse Community Center
6. Café O
7. Elixir
8. Roost
9. Rodney's Oyster Bar
10. Simply Thai
11. Curious
12. Zero Gravity
13. Cioppino's Enoteca
14. Beauty Mark
15. Blue Water Café
16. Subeez Café
17. Public Library
18. El Patio
19. Global Atomic Designs Inc.
20. Fine Finds
21. Tenthirtyeight Clothing
22. Section 3
23. Atomic Model
24. Bambu
25. Intra Venus Shoes
26. Boulangerie la Parisienne
27. Barbara-Jo's Books to Cooks
28. Glowbal Grill & Satay Bar
29. Yaletown Brewing Co.
30. Mavi Jeans

Sights
Food & Drink
Shopping
Nice to do

South Granville & Granville Island

South Granville is an area made up of just one street. That street, however, has a very chic atmosphere, with exclusive restaurants, boutiques and galleries dominating the neighborhood and expensive apartments and flats surrounding them.

The atmosphere on Granville Island is very different than on South Granville. What was once an industrial island has now become an island for artists. You'll find countless galleries and ateliers in converted factories and you'll be able to watch the artists at work. As far as theater activity, this island is more alive than ever with dance, dramatic arts and improvisation evenings all on offer. It is not surprising then, that Vancouver's art academy is located on Granville Island.

4

With so many restaurants and the large covered market, there's always something fun to do on Granville Island. Wander along the water and comb through the galleries to get a sense of the place. Since most of the island lies on the water, you can take a small ferry from the mainland to Granville Island.

6 Musts!

Gallery Row

Encourage your artistic eye

Island Park Walk

Get some fresh air

Rail Spur Alley

Wander through more galleries

Stock Market

Have a bowl of soup

False Creek Ferries

Take a ferry ride

Bard on the Beach

Watch a performance

- Sights
- Shopping
- Food & Drink
- Nice to do

⑩ FLOATING HOMES

Sights

⑥ Vancouver's **Gallery Row** lies at the foot of the Granville Bridge. You can explore about fifteen different galleries, each with its own style. Many of these galleries often show work by Canadian artists, which is a good way to get an overview of local talent.
at the foot of granville bridge, most galleries closed on monday, entrance free, bus 8 granville

⑦ Every gallery on Gallery Row has its own unique style. **Jacana**, for example, combines Asian antiques with modern art. It might sound strange, but you'd be surprised how well these two styles go together.
2435 granville street, telephone (604) 879-9306, www.jacanagallery.com, open tue-sat 10am-6pm, sun noon-5pm, entrance free, bus 8 granville

⑧ The **Douglas Reynolds Gallery** presents native art of the Canadian North coast. Find out more about the indigenous tribes of the continent by studying totem poles, masks and jewelry. Art of this quality can otherwise only be found in museums.
2335 granville street, telephone (604) 731-9292, www.douglasreynoldsgallery.com, open mon-sat 10am-6pm, sun noon-5pm, entrance free, bus 8 granville

⑩ Walking around Granville Island, you'll see a harbor on the right with houses floating on planks. These houses, also called **Floating Homes**, are very colorful and generally made of wood. Each has its own individual style.
near the granville island hotel, not open to the public, bus 8 granville

⑫ **Rail Spur Alley** is another area on Granville Island filled with art galleries. The art here varies in caliber and features a lot of ceramics, glasswork and smaller artistic objects. Make sure you visit this street as it has not yet been discovered by tourists.
opening times and telephone numbers vary, bus 8 granville

㉗ The **Vancouver Museum** has an extensive collection of art related to the history of the city of Vancouver and its surrounding areas. In the museum, you can learn about the art and history of the indigenous people who played a large role in the development of British Columbia.
1100 chestnut street, telephone (604) 736-4431, www.vanmuseum.bc.ca, open tue-wed, fri-sun 10am-5pm, thu 10am-9pm, entrance adults $10, children up to 4 free, ages 5-18 $6, bus 2 macdonald

㉘ Learn about outer space at the **H.R. MacMillan Space Center**. Take a multimedia journey through space or admire Canada's space station. This is an especially good stop for children.
1100 chestnut street, telephone (604) 738-7827, www.hrmacmillanspacecentre.com, open tue-sun 10am-5pm, entrance adults $13.50, children, students and seniors $10.50, bus 2 macdonald

㉙ The **Maritime Museum** is filled with treasures of the ocean, wreckage from lost ships, high-tech diving suits and journals from old ships. Kids will really enjoy the special activities - and don't miss out on the Pirate's cave!
1905 ogden avenue, telephone (604) 257-8300, www.vmm.bc.ca, open summer daily 10am-5pm, winter tue-sat 10am-5pm, sun noon-5pm, entrance adults $8, children, students and seniors $5.50, bus 2 macdonald

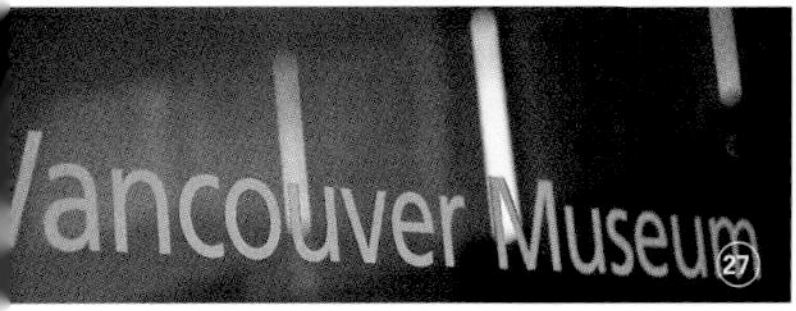
Vancouver Museum
27

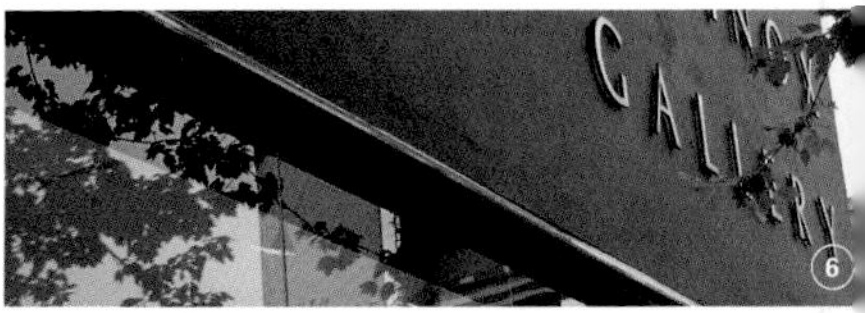
GALLERY
6

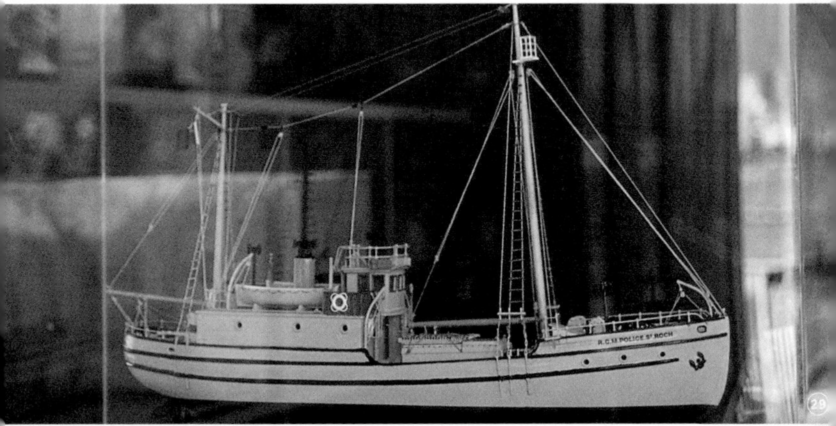
29

Food & Drink

① **Ouisi** is a good place for lunch or dinner. The food is generally quite hot here, so be prepared for spice! Favorite ingredients include turmeric and saffron, giving the food a Spanish/Mexican flavor. Try the jambalaya...
3014 granville street, telephone (604) 732-7550, open mon-wed 11am-midnight, thu-fri 11am-1am, sat 9am-1am, sun 9am-midnight, price $20, bus 8 granville

③ **West**, with its chic atmosphere and modern feel, epitomizes this neighborhood. The dishes are practically works of art. Early birds who dine before 6pm can experience the three-course menu at a discounted price.
2881 granville street, telephone (604) 738-8938, open mon-tue 5.30pm-midnight, wed-sun 11.30am-midnight, price $30, bus 8 granville

⑬ An American woman once won a million dollars from a mayonnaise company for her recipe for ciabatta with chicken. **Kharma Kitchen** now owns that recipe, and claims to be the most popular sandwich shop in town. See for yourself by having a nice lunch or cup of coffee.
1363 railspur alley, telephone (604) 647-1363, open daily 8.30am-5pm, price ciabatta $7, bus 8 granville

⑭ For a yummy drink or snack and a rest from all the sightseeing, go to **Cat's Meow**. You are sure to come across something delicious on the menu, like the stuffed Mediterranean chicken.
1540 old bridge street, telephone (604) 647-2287, open sat-thu 11am-midnight, fri-sat 11am-1am, price dinner $14, bus 8 granville

㉔ **Bridges** is the most popular restaurant on Granville Island, where you can get the fanciest hamburger and french fries. For a cheaper meal, go to the café and bistro at the back of the restaurant. The terrace overlooks the water and has a fantastic view.
1696 duranleau street, telephone (604) 687-4400, open mon-sat 11am-midnight, sun 10.30am-midnight, price restaurant $20, pub $12, bus 8 granville

21
3
1
bridges
seabird
24
lounge & eatery
STELLA ARTOIS
14

PASTA
and
SAUCES
SANDWICH
EXPRESS
COOKIES
and
ASIAN/INDIAN
and
CRACKERS
BREADS

(2) **MEINHARDT**

Shopping

(2) For the best cup of coffee you've ever had in a supermarket, go to **Meinhardt**. This supermarket has a fresh sandwich department, where you can buy delicious, ready-made meals for a quick lunch or dinner. You'll find a lot of European brands on the shelves here as well.
3002 granville street, telephone (604) 732-4405, open mon-sat 8am-9pm, sun 9am-9pm, bus 8 granville

(4) You could spend hours walking around **Caban**, a home furnishings store brought to you by Canada's own Club Monaco. This store has simple, stylish accessories and furniture for every room in the home.
2912 granville street, telephone (604) 742-1522, open mon-wed, sat-sun 10am-7pm, thu-fri 10am-9pm, bus 8 granville

(5) The largest bookstore chain in Canada, **Chapters**, is a nice place to browse, leaf through books before you buy them and enjoy a cup of coffee. Most stores have comfortable chairs scattered throughout them, so you can take your time leafing through the books and magazines.
2505 granville street, telephone (604) 731-7822, open daily 9am-11pm, bus 8 granville

(11) **Opus** is the best place in Vancouver for artist's supplies for painting, modeling or drawing. Granville Island is the perfect environment for this store, which also sells the most beautiful paint boxes.
1360 johnston street, telephone (604) 666-6477, open mon-fri 8.30am-6pm, sat 9am-6pm, sun 10am-6pm, bus 8 granville

(15) Children go wild when parents take them to the **Kids Market**. You can buy all sorts of toys here and the place is overflowing with activity and youthful energy. Luckily there's a normal entrance for adults next to the special, smaller children's entrance.
1496 cartwright street, telephone (604) 689-8447, open daily 10am-6pm, bus 8 granville

(17) At **Paper-Ya** you'll discover lovely paper and parchment from all over the world. Huge wooden drawers hold packing paper, parchment and paper that feels like fabric. There are also shelves full of diaries and notebooks that are so nice you'll wish you were a great writer!
net loft building 9, 1666 johnston street, telephone (604) 684-2531, open daily 10am-6pm, bus 8 granville

(18) If you want to buy unique postcards, there's a good chance you'll find what you're looking for at **Postcard Place**. This tiny shop has literally hundreds of cards.
net loft building 11, 1666 johnston street, telephone (604) 684-6909, open daily 10am-6pm, bus 8 granville

(19) Stringing beads and making your own jewelry can be fun, and at **Beadworks** you can learn how it's done. You'll certainly be inspired by the thousands of beads in this store, which fit in perfectly with the artsy atmosphere of Granville Island.
net loft building 5, 1666 johnston street, telephone (604) 682-2323, open daily 10am-6pm, bus 8 granville

(20) Everything in **Circle Craft** is handmade by artists from British Columbia. Different forms of arts and crafts are represented here, from glassblowing to ceramics. The store is filled with unique objects.
net loft building 1, 1666 johnston street, telephone (604) 669-8021, open daily 10am-6pm, bus 8 granville

(21) Feel like going on a picnic? Go to **Public Market** for all the ingredients. You can get fresh fruit, meats and fish, as well as baked goods, Italian delicacies and wine. This covered market is always busy - not surprising, since the food here is much more delicious than from the supermarket!
1689 johnston street, telephone (604) 666-6477, open daily 9am-6pm, bus 8 granville

(22) When you're in the Public Market, stop by the **Stock Market** for the best soups and sauces. The ready-made soups can be eaten at the bar or taken to go.
1689 johnston street, telephone (604) 687-2433, open daily 9am-6pm, bus 8 granville

㉓ All the ingredients for a wonderful Asian meal are available at **South China Seas Trading Co**. For inspiration, leaf through the cookbooks at the back of the shop.
1689 johnston street, telephone (604) 681-5402, open daily 9am-6pm, bus 8 granville

ISLAND PARK WALK
9
9
9
16

Nice to do

(9) **Island Park Walk** is a great place for a quiet stroll or a jog. The path takes you all over Granville Island, mostly following the water or sometimes the harbor.
path begins on your right when you arrive at granville island (follow the signs), bus 8 granville

(16) Learn how to make beer at the small **Granville Island Brewery**, which offers tours and tastings. If you don't feel like going on a tour, just go straight to the 'tap room'.
1441 cartwright street, telephone (604) 687-2739, open daily 10am-7pm, price of tour $8, bus 8 granville

(25) You can sail in little ferryboats to the West End from Granville Island. Many residents of Vancouver use this as a practical means of transport, but the **False Creek Ferries** are so nice you might want to make the crossing just for fun. You can also get to the beach this way.
1804 boatlift lane, telephone (604) 684-7781,
www.granvilleislandferries.bc.ca, open daily, boats leave every 5-30 min from 10am-6pm or 10pm depending on destination, price ticket $3, bus 8 granville

(26) **Vanier Park** is great for a walk, a picnic or an afternoon of museum-hopping. The park lies at the foot of the Burrard Bridge and has a spectacular view of Vancouver's skyline. You can also get here on one of the small ferries.
1100 chestnut street, entrance free, bus 2 macdonald

(25) FALSE CREEK FERRIES

30 Every year at the beginning of the summer, **Bard on the Beach** begins its summer program. Each year a few of Shakespeare's works are performed in the open air of Vanier Park. This is a professional theater and a thoroughly enjoyable spectacle.
vanier park, telephone (604) 739-0559, www.bardonthebeach.org,
open beginning of june-end of september, entrance $20, bus 2 macdonald

South Granville & Granville Island

WALKING TOUR 4

Be advised: Don't walk this route on a Monday, because many of the galleries will be closed.

Take bus 8 in the direction of Granville and get off at the intersection of Granville Street and Fifteenth Avenue. Stay on Granville Street and walk to the left (1) (2) (3). You can do a bit of shopping here and there on Granville Street (4) (5), but the selection really picks up when you go down Gallery Row (6) (7) (8) to visit some of the galleries. Right before the bridge, turn left through the pedestrian's subway. Keep to the right of the tunnel. After the steps, walk left through the park and cross the road at the traffic lights. Keep following this street until you leave Granville Island. Turn left on to the first path and enjoy a walk around the island (9). Go left into the street across from the floating houses (10), where you can browse at Opus (11). Go left at Johnston Street and take your first left. Then take your first left again and wander along the galleries in Rail Spur Alley (12). For a sandwich or a cookie, try Kharma Kitchen (13). At the end of the street, follow the sharp curve (14) (15) (16). Cross over to the right and take the first street to the left. Go into the Net Loft Building to visit some interesting little shops (17) (18) (19) (20). You will see the Public Market at the exit (21) (22). Get inspired at South China Seas Trading Co to cook something delicious (23). Watch out, you can easily get lost in this covered market. From almost every exit you can see the Bridges (24) restaurant where you can enjoy a drink. Now you can do two things: walk to a ferryboat in the small harbor (25) to cross over to the other side and spend the rest of the day resting on the beach of English Bay; or walk back to the Island Park Walk and follow the path to the right. Finally you come out in Vanier Park (26) where you can visit three different museums (27) (28) (29) and where you can enjoy performances from Bard on the Beach (30) Follow the boulevard in the direction of Kitsilano Beach, where you can wait for a bus on Cornwall Street to get back to your hotel.

Sights
Food & Drink
Shopping
Nice to do
START
FINISH
FINISH
OPTIE 1
OPTIE 2
Pacific Spacecentre & Vancouver Museum
Granville Island Public Market
Art Club Theatre
Ferry Ramp
Ogden Ave
McNicoll Ave
Whyte Ave
Creelman Ave
Burrard St
Greer Ave
Cornwall Ave
York Ave
1 Ave W
2 Ave W
3 Ave W
4 Ave W
5 Ave W
6 Ave W
7 Ave W
8 Ave W
Broadway W
10 Ave W
11 Ave W
12 Ave W
13 Ave W
14 Ave W
15 Ave W
16 Ave W
17 Ave W
18 Ave W
Marstrand Ave
Redbud Ln
Salal Dr
Cedar Cres
Arbutus St
Laburnum St
Walnut St
Cypress St
Chestnut St
Maple St
Vine St
Yew St
Pine St
Fir St
East Blvd
GRANVILLE ST
Hemlock St
Birch St
Alder St
Spruce St
Oak St
Laurel St
Creekside Dr
Pennyfarthing Dr
Mariner Walk
Duranleau St
Johnston St
Old Bridge St
Cartwright St
Old Bridge Walk
Fountain Way
Birch Walk
Alder Bay Walk
Park Walk
Lameys Mill Rd
Island Park Walk
Alder Cross
The Castings
Forge Walk
Sitka Sq
Scantlings
The Ironwork Passage
Charleson Rd
Marpole Ave
McRae Ave
Wolfe Ave
Tecumseh Ave
The Crescent
Richelieu Ave
Beach Ave
Thurlow St
Harwood St
Burnaby St
Hornby St
Davie St
Granville St
Howe St
HOWE ST
Pacific St
Drake St
SEYMOUR ST
Richards St
Homer St
Helmcken St
99

1. Ouisi
2. Meinhardt
3. West
4. Caban
5. Chapters
6. Gallery Row
7. Jacana
8. Douglas Reynolds Gallery
9. Island Park Walk
10. Floating Homes
11. Opus
12. Rail Spur Alley
13. Kharma Kitchen
14. Cat's Meow
15. Kids Market
16. Granville Island Brewery
17. Paper-Ya
18. Postcard Place
19. Beadworks
20. Circle Craft
21. Public Market
22. Stock Market
23. South China Seas Trading Co.
24. Bridges
25. False Creek Ferries
26. Vanier Park
27. Vancouver Museum
28. H.R. MacMillan Space Center
29. Maritime Museum
30. Bard on the Beach

Sights
Food & Drink
Shopping
Nice to do

Kitsilano

Kitsilano (or 'Kits') is a quiet area near University of British Columbia where lots of young families and students live. Its large, old residences were built mainly circa the 1920s in accordance with principles of 'Craftsman Architecture.'

The two main streets in Kitsilano are West Broadway and West Fourth Avenue, great places for shopping, eating and going out. Both streets are very busy on weekend mornings, when people are out for breakfast and coffee.

5

The beaches in Kitsilano are a big attraction in the summer. Jericho Beach is a bit quieter, and mainly visited by families while Kitsilano Beach is where young people sunbathe, play beach volleyball and toss frisbees.

In the 60s, Kitsilano was home to a lot of hippies, and evidence of this still exists in the numerous organic shops in the area. Other than this, however, hippy culture has pretty much disappeared and now University students and the occasional yuppie set the pace of the neighborhood.

6 Musts!

Disc Golf

Play a round of Disc Golf

Craftsmen Architecture

Admire this unique style

East is East

Taste the exotic flavors

Kidsbooks

Browse through the wonderful selection of children's books

Sophie's Cosmic Café

The most famous breakfast in Kitsilano

Kitsilano Beach

Sunbathe, swim or just rest

- Sights
- Shopping
- Food & Drink
- Nice to do

CRAFTSMEN ARCHITECTURE ⑲

Sights

⑲ Architecture buffs will love the old houses in Kitsilano, which follow a style that came about in the 1920s known as **Craftsman Architecture** or California Bungalow Architecture. According to Craftsman principles, houses are built with balconies, verandas and often with cement pillars. On Stephens Street between 7th and 8th Avenues are some of the most admirable examples of these houses.
2200-block on stephens street, not open to the public, bus 10 ubc

⑳ Hidden on a side street, you'll find Vancouver's **Most Beautiful Block**. This row of terracotta-colored houses with lovely gardens has earned this title three years in a row and everyone will definitely agree the attractive block deserves it!
2000-block on trafalgar street, not open to the public, bus 4 ubc

㉕ The **Arbutus Market** was opened to shoppers in 1907 and is now a place for a cup of coffee and a sandwich. The building is still in its original state, and on the façade you can see remnants of the oldest supermarket in Kitsilano.
2200 arbutus street, telephone (604) 736-5644, open mon-fri 6am-6pm, sat-sun 9am-6pm, price coffee $2, bus 10 ubc

ARBUTUS
REAL MARKET FOODS
25
MOCHA
25
20

8
MEDITERRANEAN
DELI
7
EASTERN SHAKES
9
The Fringe
10

Food & Drink

(3) After a walk on the beach or a round of disc golf (played with Frisbees), catch your breath at **Cuppa Joe**. Order your coffee 'iced' or warm and sit on the roof terrace or enjoy the funky interior with green and red velvet chairs and couches.
3744 west 4th avenue, telephone (604) 224-3687, open daily 6am-11pm, price coffee $1.55, bus 4 powell

(7) In the hustle and bustle of West Broadway there's a small restaurant with delicious Persian, Afghan and Indian food. The interior of **East is East** is dark, and you'll sit on heavy wooden stools at tables often shared with other guests. You can also enjoy a more romantic setting by eating in one of the sections curtained off from the rest of the restaurant. These can be reserved during the week, but unfortunately not on weekends.
3243 west broadway, telephone (604) 715-7747, open mon-sat 11am-11pm, sun noon-10pm, price $9, bus 10 ubc

(8) This part of West Broadway is a Greek neighborhood, with quite a few Greek restaurants and even a Greek bank. For a good cup of coffee or a meal and some groceries, try **Minerva's Mediterranean Deli**.
3207 west broadway, telephone (604) 733-3954, open daily 8am-8pm, bus 10 ubc

(9) If you don't watch out, you might walk right by this small restaurant. **Fiction** is a neighborhood café, tastefully decorated with large paintings on the wall - a perfect restaurant for a romantic dinner. It's also a late night hotspot. On weekends enjoy a hearty breakfast here. The martinis and tapas are the most popular items on the menu.
3162 west broadway, telephone (604) 736-7576, open mon-fri 5.30pm-2am, sat-sun 10am-2am, price $20, bus 10 ubc

(10) A beer and a snack is the best thing to order at **Fringe**, where the interior reminds you that you're in a neighborhood café. The beer tastes best at the bar and the clippings on the bulletin board serve as a good catalyst for a political discussion. You can also dine, but don't expect 'haute cuisine.'
3124 west broadway, telephone (604) 738-6977, open mon-fri 3pm-2am, sat-sun 1pm-2am, price $8, bus 10 ubc

(11) **Vertical**, one restaurant that stays open late, has delicious pizzas baked in a wood-fired oven. Ask about the specials, or try the fantastic Sunday buffet brunch - you're guaranteed to not be hungry for the rest of the day.
3116 west broadway, telephone (604) 737-2181, open mon-sat noon-2am, sun 11am-1am, price $20, bus 10 ubc

(14) **Glacé** - a Frozen Cakery is full of ice cream cakes. If you can't handle a whole cake, treat yourself to a slice, a shake or a delicious ice cream. Your mouth will definitely start watering as soon as you enter. This is also a great place to go for dessert after dinner.
3073 west broadway, telephone (604) 733-7889, open daily noon-9pm, price slice of cake $3, bus 10 ubc

(15) **Calhoun's** serves delicious coffee, cappuccino, cookies and sandwiches 24 hours a day and is always full of customers. With large tables and lots of newspapers and magazines to read, you'll be tempted to stay all day.
3035 west broadway, telephone (604) 737-7062, open 24 hours daily, price coffee $2, bus 10 ubc

(16) The current trend of eating organic and natural foods is alive and well in Kitsilano, where there are plenty of places to get an organic meal. The salads sold at **Fuel - Natural Eatery** are particularly delicious. You can eat in or order it 'to go.'
2967 west broadway, telephone (604) 736-3835, open mon-sat 11am-7pm, closed sunday, price $7, bus 10 ubc

CALHOUN'S
Coffee
15
16

㉛ TANGERINE

(21) Fusion cooking has become very popular in Vancouver, as it has elsewhere in the world. **Chivana**, a combination of Cuban and Asian ingredients, is one place to experience these new flavors. It doesn't really matter what you order here, you'll be pleasantly surprised.
2340 west 4th avenue, telephone (604) 733-0330, open mon-thu 5pm-1am, fri 5pm-2am, sat noon-2am, sun noon-midnight, price $15, bus 10 ubc

(24) The city's most popular place for breakfast on weekends is **Sophie's Cosmic Café**. Besides the delicious food with creative names, the interior is very unique. Order a big shake to start, but expect a bit of a wait on weekends.
2095 west 4th avenue, telephone (604) 732-681, open daily 8am-9.30pm, price breakfast $8, bus 10 ubc

(27) **Taka Sushi** is a good choice if you want to try a Japanese restaurant offering more than sushi. Order a delicious Japanese barbecue dish instead. Take your time for dinner, because it can sometimes take a while for your order to arrive.
2059 west 4th avenue, telephone (604) 734-4990, open tue-fri noon-2pm, 5pm-10pm, sat-sun 5pm-10pm, price $15, bus 4 ubc

(28) The margaritas at **Las Margaritas** are the best. This Mexican restaurant serves jugfuls of delicious drinks in all kinds of fruit flavors. On the terrace, which is decorated in authentic Mexican style, you can enjoy the sun, a drink and great Mexican food.
1999 west 4th avenue, telephone (604) 734-7117, open mon-thu 11am-10pm, fri 11am-11pm, sat 5.30pm-midnight, sun 5.30pm-10pm, price $10, bus 4 ubc

(31) **Tangerine** prepares exciting dishes with Asian ingredients that taste absolutely fantastic. This is a very trendy restaurant with a stylish interior. The lounge-style background music helps complete the picture.
1685 yew street, telephone (604) 739-4018, open daily 5pm-midnight, weekend brunch sat-sun 9am-3pm, price $20, bus 4 ubc

Shopping

④ There are a few great second-hand clothing stores on Fourth Avenue, like **Fourteen Plus** where you can get clothes in bigger sizes.
3636 west 4th avenue, telephone (604) 731-9975, open sun-mon noon-5pm, tue-sat 10.30am-5.30pm, bus 4 ubc

⑤ **Happy Kids**, will make even the most finicky kids happy with its selection of very nice children's clothes. Happy 3 for adults is right next door. Everything is second-hand, so it's wonderfully cheap!
3635-3629 west 4th avenue, telephone (604) 733-9638, open mon-sat noon-6pm, sun noon-5pm, bus 4 ubc

⑥ The **Blue Room** has lots of shoes and jewelry in addition to second-hand clothing. In this dreamy interior you'll certainly find a host of must-haves!
3570 west 4th avenue, telephone (604) 732-4286, open mon-sat 11am-6pm, sun noon-5pm, bus 4 ubc

⑬ At **Kids Books** you can be a kid again, as you discover all the books you loved as a child. You'll most probably end up browsing here for longer than you had planned. The lovely interior and fantastic selection of books makes it difficult to get rid of customers.
3083 west broadway, telephone (604) 738-5335, open mon-thu 9.30am-6pm, fri 9.30am-9pm, sat 9.30am-6pm, sun noon-5pm, bus 10 ubc

⑰ The **Candy Aisle** is another throwback to your youth. All the candy you thought had disappeared can be found in this store and it's great fun to be buying candy in a shop with bright green and purple walls and Abba playing in the background.
2887 west broadway, telephone (604) 689-3330, open mon-thu 10am-6pm, wed-sat 10am-9pm, sun noon-6pm, bus 10 ubc

4
6
22
17
18
13
Philadelphia Chickens

(30) LIQUID

(18) For trendy brands and cool shoes go to **Plenty** where, in addition to clothes for men and women, you'll find nice presents, books and cards. Everything here is hip and stylish.
2803 west broadway, telephone (604) 736-4484, open mon-wed 10am-6pm, thu-fri 10am-9pm, sat 10am-6pm, sun noon-6pm, bus 10 ubc

(22) Shop at **Mexican Arte** and buy nice glasses, cups and platters. The Mexican owner imports everything straight from the homeland.
2242 west 4th avenue, telephone (604) 739-1767, open mon-sat 10am-6pm, sun noon-5pm, bus 4 ubc

(23) From picture frames to martini glasses, from diaries to tiles with proverbs written on them, **Hope Unlimited** has loads of great gift ideas. You will easily find something small for yourself or for someone else.
2206 west 4th avenue, telephone (604) 732-4438, open mon-fri 10am-8pm, sat 10am-6pm, sun 11am-6pm, bus 4 ubc

(26) The ultimate summer sport in Vancouver is Ultimate Frisbee, where one team has to try to catch a Frisbee within an end zone - a bit like Rugby or American Football. **Gaya** is the place to go for the ultimate outfit. They've got more than just sportswear at this shop.
2077 west 4th avenue, telephone (604) 834-6289, open (may-sep) sat-wed 10am-6pm, thu-fri 10am-9pm, bus 4 ubc

(29) **Moule** is the sort of store where you look but don't buy. You'll see the most beautiful watches, clothes, salt-and-pepper shakers and home accessories, but after you see the prices you might think twice about making a purchase.
1994 west 4th avenue, telephone (604) 732-4066, open mon-thu 10am-6pm, fri 10am-8pm, sat 10am-6pm, sun noon-6pm, bus 4 ubc

(30) **Liquid** sells women's clothing designed by local talent. In addition to t-shirts, the store sells more unique pieces. It is nice to have a look around and discover what the fashion designers of Vancouver have to offer.
2050 west 4th avenue, telephone (604) 737-1600, open mon-sat 11am-6pm, sun noon-5.30, bus 4 ubc

Nice to do

(1) **Jericho Beach** is one of the most beautiful beaches in Vancouver and has a fantastic view of the center of the city. Swimming is safe here, and this is also a nice place to go for walks.
at the foot of alma street, bus 4 bianca

(2) Start the day with some activity! In Vancouver there are quite a few **Disc Golf** courses where you can play for free (the Jericho Beach park has one of them). Take your own discs with you (a Frisbee is also allowed) and try with three or four good throws to get the disc into the metal bucket. It's the perfect way to relax in a busy city.
jericho beach park near the jericho hill center, www.bcdss.bc.ca, free entrance, take your own discs with you, bus 4 bianca

(12) Check out the **Hollywood Theatre** to see if there's anything interesting playing. This cinema shows second-run films before they go to video and on weekends has children's matinees.
3123 west broadway, telephone (604) 738-3211, www.hollywoodtheatre.ca, open matinee 1pm, evening showing 7.30pm, entrance $5 for two films, bus 10 ubc

(32) At the end of the day, take a walk, play beach volleyball or laze about on **Kitsilano Beach**. You can also enjoy the sunset from this beach, and if you're lucky, you might see some seals and sea otters swimming around.
cornwall street, bus 2 macdonald

32
2
32
1

Kitsilano

WALKING TOUR 5

Take bus 4 in the direction of Bianca and get off at Jericho Beach 1. Throw a few holes at the disc golf course 2 or go for a walk on the beach. Afterwards, walk east to West Fourth Avenue and have a rest from all of the activity at Cuppa Joe 3. A bit further up you'll find a few nice second-hand shops 4 5 6, which you should definitely check out. Go right on Blenheim Street, then left to West Broadway. In this street you can have something delicious to eat 7 8 9 10 11 14 15 16, go out 12 and shop 13 17 18. As far as restaurants go, you can find everything here, from Greek to Japanese or Continental. After you've had enough of shopping and looking around, turn left on Stephens Street where, on your right hand side, you can see examples of the authentic Craftsman Architecture 19. Turn right on Seventh Avenue and directly left on Trafalgar Street for the most beautiful street in Vancouver 20. Turn right on Fifth Avenue and enjoy more of the architecture. Turn left on Balsam and right on West Fourth Avenue, where there's lots to do. Choose from many restaurants 21 24 27 28 and shops 22 23 26 29 30. For the oldest supermarket, which is now a coffee shop, go right on Arbutus till you get to Sixth Avenue. You'll see Arbutus Market 25 on the corner. Afterwards, walk back to Fourth Avenue and turn right. On Maple Street turn right and enjoy the view as you walk down a steep hill. Turn left at First Avenue and right on Yew Street. This is where the area of Kitsilano began long ago. For a delicious dinner of exciting Asian cuisine go to Tangerine 31. Walk further down the hill, where you'll come out on Kitsilano Beach 32.

START
FINISH
Kitsilano Beach
Old Hastings Mill Store
1
2
3
4
5
6
7
8
9
10
11
12
13
14
15
16
17
18
19
20
21
22
23
24
25
26
27
28
29
30
31
32
Sights
Food & Drink
Shopping
Nice to do
Cameron Ave
Point Grey Rd
Cornwall Ave
York Ave
1 Ave W
2 Ave W
3 Ave W
4 Ave W
5 Ave W
6 Ave W
7 Ave W
8 Ave W
Broadway W
10 Ave W
11 Ave W
12 Ave W
13 Ave W
14 Ave W
15 Ave W
16 Ave W
17 Ave W
18 Ave W
19 Ave W
20 Ave W
21 Ave W
22 Ave W
23 Ave W
24 Ave W
King Edward Ave W
26 Ave W
27 Ave W
Wallace St
Alma St
Dunbar St
Collingwood St
Waterloo St
Blenheim St
Trutch St
Balaclava St
Bayswater St
Macdonald St
Stephens St
Trafalgar St
Larch St
Balsam St
Vine St
Yew St
Arbutus St
Highbury St
Ghent Ln
Ortona Cres
Antwerp Ln
Crown St
Crown Cres
Wallace Cres
Camosun St
Dunbar Divers
Kitsilano Divers
Carnarvon St
Mackenzie St
Marstrand Ave
11 Ave W
Redbud Ln
Salal Dr
Quadra St
Quesnel Dr
Galiano Dr
Puget Dr
Valdez Rd
Valley Dr
East Blvd
Alamein Ave
Oliver Cres
McBain Ave
Parkway Dr
Dunkirk St

1. Jericho Beach
2. Disc Golf
3. Cuppa Joe
4. Fourteen Plus
5. Happy Kids
6. Blue Room
7. East is East
8. Minerva's Mediterranean Deli
9. Fiction
10. Fringe
11. Vertical
12. Hollywood Theatre
13. Kids Books
14. Glacé
15. Calhoun's
16. Fuel - Natural Eatery
17. Candy Aisle
18. Plenty
19. Craftsman Architecture
20. Most Beautiful Block
21. Chivana
22. Mexican Arte
23. Hope Unlimited
24. Sophie's Cosmic Café
25. Arbutus Market
26. Gaya
27. Taka Sushi
28. Las Margaritas
29. Moule
30. Liquid
31. Tangerine
32. Kitsilano Beach

- **Sights**
- **Food & Drink**
- **Shopping**
- **Nice to do**

Main Street & Commercial Drive

Main Street separates east and west Vancouver. This wide street runs right across Vancouver, but the best part of it begins south of the city center. This area only started to get popular in the 1970s, when people discovered how cheap it was to buy the old Victorian houses there. Young couples began to move in and restore the houses to their former glory.

At the same time, Main Street became a popular location for designers and artists, who began opening shops and galleries. Today, this is a paradise for lovers of interior and fashion design. Additionally, you'll find the best second-hand stores, many antiques and fantastic restaurants.

6

Commercial Drive is east of Main Street. After the Second World War, this area was dubbed Little Italy because of all of the Italian immigrants who settled there. The name has since disappeared, but you'll still find a lot of restaurants serving real Italian coffee and cappuccino. Commercial Drive, or 'the Drive' for short, is a mix of different cultures. This is especially recognizable in the restaurants, which serve specialties from all over the world.

On Main Street and Commercial Drive life revolves around drinking coffee, eating good food and appreciating art. You might not come across many cultural sights here, but you will get a taste of a special atmosphere you won't find anywhere else!

6 Musts!

Antique Row

Wander along Main Street

The Reef

Eat Caribbean food

Davis Houses

Admire the houses on West 10th avenue

Yogi's

Enjoy Indian food

Libra Room

Italian coffee and a delicious panini

Magpie

Look for your favorite magazine

- **Sights**
- **Shopping**
- **Food & Drink**
- **Nice to do**

HERITAGE HALL ⑫

Sights

⑫ The building now called **Heritage Hall** used to be 'Postal Station C.' The city council, convinced that Vancouver would extend in the direction of Main Street, built this beautiful neo-classical building in 1915 as the middle point of the new uptown. Unfortunately, Main Street didn't become the neighborhood they expected, and only the ground floor was ever used as a post office.
3102 main street, telephone (604) 879-4816, not open to the public, bus 3 main

⑬ One of the attractions of Main Street are the beautiful, restored Victorian houses. The two most famous houses, known as the **Davis Houses**, can be found on West 10th Avenue. The bright colors of these houses are surprising and their architecture is extraordinary.
117 west 10th avenue, not open to the public, bus 9 broadway station

⑭ It is hard to imagine that, in 1912, the **Lee Building** was the first skyscraper in Vancouver. The building only has seven floors! Today there are a few shops on the ground floor with offices on the floors above.
175 west broadway, upper floors not open to the public, bus 9 broadway station

15
16
café deux soleils
LOCUS
CAFE
41
21
3
4
15

Food & Drink

(2) With its colorful interior and rhythmic music, **The Reef** sets a truly tropical scene. The menu features delicious dishes from the Caribbean and the cook, who comes from Jamaica, works his magic in the kitchen with wonderful herbs and ingredients. The Jerk Chicken is definitely recommended.
4172 main street, telephone (604) 874-5375, open mon-fri 11am-midnight, sat-sun 10am-midnight, price $11, bus 3 main

(3) Come to **Locus** on the first Monday of every month and you'll get a free glass of wine while experiencing the unveiling of the newest art installation. This artistic restaurant has a fabulous ambiance and you can be sure to find something you like on the extensive menu.
4121 main street, telephone (604) 708-4121, open daily 10am-2am, price $12, bus 3 main

(4) Like so many restaurants on Main Street, the walls of the **Liberty Bakery** feature a frequent rotation of new art. Drink your coffee outside, or head inside where a collection of different tables and chairs creates a rustic look. This is also a great place to get a delicious sandwich, but keep in mind that only cash is accepted.
3699 main street, telephone (604) 709-9999, open mon 7am-6pm, tue 8am-4pm, wed-fri 7am-6pm, sat 7am-5pm, sun 8am-5pm, price coffee $2, bus 3 main

(15) On Commercial Drive coffee culture prevails. There is a coffee shop on almost every corner of the street, and at the hip **J.J. Bean House of Coffee** you can even drink organic coffee. Order a healthy muffin while you read one of the papers that are spread out over the tables.
2206 commercial drive, telephone (604) 254-3723, open sun-wed 7am-8pm, thu-sat 7am-10.30pm, price coffee $2, skytrain broadway station

(16) When you walk into **Café Deux Soleil** it might take a minute to get used to the interior. The large room with tables and chairs scattered here and there has a serious atmosphere, and attracts an interesting mix of families and students. Every Wednesday is reggae night.
2096 commercial drive, telephone (604) 254-1195, daily 8am-midnight, price $8, bus 3 main

(17) The bright, colorful interior of **Clove** is the perfect place to enjoy delicious Thai specialties. The fresh colors and lounge music provide an apt setting for Thai food, and the restaurant is famous for its 'lassi', a mango shake-like drink. Try the phad thai, too.
2054 commercial drive, telephone (604) 255-5550, open mon-sat 5pm-midnight, price $12, skytrain broadway

(18) In North America, fries are usually served with ketchup, but at **Belgian Fries** they come in a pointed paper sack with lots of delicious mayonnaise on the side. It's the way fries are meant to be served!
1885 commercial drive, telephone (604) 253-4220, open daily 11.30am-10pm, price $4, skytrain broadway

(19) **Wasubeez** is a popular place to study or work while enjoying breakfast or a cup of coffee. There is usually a table available, at breakfast, lunch or dinner. At night, try the fries with garlic mayonnaise and the 'Chicken WaZuBwich' for a delicious, fast meal. The huge, colorful mural on the wall is a picture of the city in Italy where the owner grew up.
1622 commercial drive, telephone (604) 253-5299, open mon-sat 11.30am-1am, sun 11am-midnight, price $12, skytrain broadway

(20) For coffee and a delicious panini, go to **Libra Room**, a cozy restaurant with a huge fireplace in the middle, where you can order coffee from the Italian owner and his mother. The panini with grilled eggplant and mozzarella are particularly delicious. You can also sprawl out on a comfortable couch to enjoy your coffee.
1608 commercial drive, telephone (604) 255-3787, open sun-mon 9am-9pm, tue-sat 9am-midnight, price $12, skytrain broadway

(21) At **Bukowski's** you'll never get bored during a meal. This restaurant is famous for its jazz nights, when live bands perform. On other days, there is a DJ and once a month a burlesque dancer performs. The menu features dishes ranging from Asian and African specialties to hamburgers with fries. Don't miss this place.
1447 commercial drive, telephone (604) 253-4770, open mon-fri noon-1am, sat 10.30am-1am, sun 10.30am-midnight, price $19, skytrain broadway

(22) Enjoy delicious food in a minimalist environment at the dark and moody **Fuse**. The tapas are prepared with ingredients from Italy, France and Asia, giving them a very specific flavor. The mix-n-match pastas are very popular, allowing you to make your own combination of pasta, sauce and filling.
1438 commercial drive, telephone (604) 251-5512, open tue-wed 11am-11pm, thu-sun 11am-midnight, price $15, skytrain broadway

(23) **Juicy Lucy's** has a great selection of fresh juices - from healthy carrot-spinach-cucumber smoothies to delicious banana and strawberry drinks. Lunch is available as well, and almost all the sandwiches and shakes are vegetarian.
1420 commercial drive, telephone (604) 254-6101, open mon-sat 7am-8pm, sun 8am-8pm, price smoothie $4.50, skytrain broadway

(24) Feel like a vegetarian Indian meal? Then try **Yogi's**, where you'll discover that eating delights such as a delicious cauliflower dish doesn't have to cost a fortune. You'll smell the aroma of these Indian curry dishes long before you get to the restaurant's door.
1408 commercial drive, telephone (604) 251-9644, open mon-fri 11.30am-2.30pm, 5pm-10.30pm, sat-sun noon-11pm, price $8, skytrain broadway

(25) At **Marcello** the pizzas are prepared according to an authentic Italian recipe and then baked in a wood-fired oven. The oven sits in the middle of the restaurant and looks like a huge face, with an enormous mouth where the pizzas disappear.
1404 commercial drive, telephone (604) 215-7760, open sun-wed 11am-11pm, thu-sat 11am-midnight, price $11, skytrain broadway

(28) The hip decor of **Turks** goes well with the atmosphere on Commercial Drive. Inside, you'll find a cozy ambience and delicious coffee. Take a book and spend some time chilling out.
1276 commercial drive, telephone (604) 255-5805, open mon-fri 6.30am-11.30pm, sat-sun 7am-midnight, price coffee $2, skytrain broadway

(29) The interior of **Havana's** is based on the décor of one of Ernest Hemingway's favorite cafés in Cuba. His favorite drink, the mojito, is also available, as well as delicious Cuban dishes. The back of the restaurant houses a gallery and theater, which puts on interesting performances.
1212 commercial drive, telephone (604) 253-9119, open mon-fri 11am-midnight, sat-sun 10am-midnight, price $15, skytrain broadway

Shopping

⑥ **Front and Company** brings new life to old things. In addition to clothing, you'll find candelabras, picture frames and wine glasses. The shop is famous for its window display, which is constantly changed by the owner and always looks fantastic.
3746-3772 main street, telephone (604) 879-8205, open daily 11am-6pm, bus 3 main

⑦ **Simple** is your classic success story. The artist who opened it had just graduated and planned to continue studying when she decided to open her own shop. From that moment onward, commissions from interior designers poured in and she came up with her own line of vases, cushions and curtains. The style is as simple as the name suggests, and goes with every kind of decor.
3638 main street, telephone (604) 877-0323, open wed-sat 11am-6pm, sun noon-5pm, bus 3 main

⑧ **Smoking Lily** is a tiny store filled with colorful, printed t-shirts - most with lilies on them!
3634 main street, telephone (604) 873-5459, open mon-sat 11am-6pm, sun noon-5pm, bus 3 main

⑨ At **Eugene Choo** it's fun to discover the newest styles, generally created by fashion designers from Vancouver. You're in the right place for the latest trends and craziest clothes.
3683 main street, telephone (604) 873-8874, open mon-thu, sat 11am-6pm, fri 11am-7pm, sun noon-5pm, bus 3 main

9
6
7

26
OBSERVER
'We would welcome your troops with flowers'
In the Congo, history repeats
Women aroused by male, female images: study
27
BAKER'S DOZ
10

(10) One of the many antique shops in this neighborhood is **A Baker's Dozen**. One unique thing about it is that you can buy soapboxes and empty soap cans from the 1950s. There is a special room in the back full of antique children's toys, for real collectors. Unfortunately, the room is by appointment only but there is a window you can look through to catch a glimpse of the merchandise.
3520 main street, telephone (604) 879-3348, open mon-sat 11am-6pm, sun noon-5pm, bus 3 main

(26) For earthenware, furniture and paintings by local artists, go to **Dr. Vigari**, a good place to find a unique souvenir.
1312 commercial drive, telephone (604) 255-9513, open mon-sat 11am-6pm, sun 11am-5pm, bus 3 main

(27) **Magpie** has every magazine imaginable, from the ubiquitous Elle to independent political magazines. You'll also find interesting newspapers, including some that are hanging in the window, so you can read the latest news as you pass by.
1319 commercial drive, telephone (604) 253-6666, open mon-fri 9am-9pm, sat-sun 9am-7pm, bus 3 main

Nice to do

① Over the years, Main Street has gained fame for its **Antique Row**. As a tourist, you probably won't be buying huge pieces of furniture, but looking around can't hurt. The stock varies from antiques to curiosities and from English to Chinese showpieces.
4400-3200 block main street, www.main-street.ca, bus 3 main

⑤ If you're feeling inspired by all of the art around you, let your creativity loose at **Homeworks**. Using glass, tiles and mirrors you can create a beautiful mosaic within an hour. Simple projects include house numbers or a lovely set of coasters.
3825 main street, telephone (604) 875-1133, www.homeworksstudio.com, open tue-wed 11am-9pm, thu-sun 11am-6pm, bus 3 main

⑪ Probably the most fun to be had at a gallery in Vancouver is at the **Starving Artist**, a small space bursting with neighborhood artists. There are no rules here - any artist is allowed to sell his or her work. Look carefully and you just might discover the next Warhol or Picasso!
3243 main street, telephone (604) 874-2781, open mon-fri 9am-7pm, sat 10am-6pm, sun noon-5pm, bus 3 main

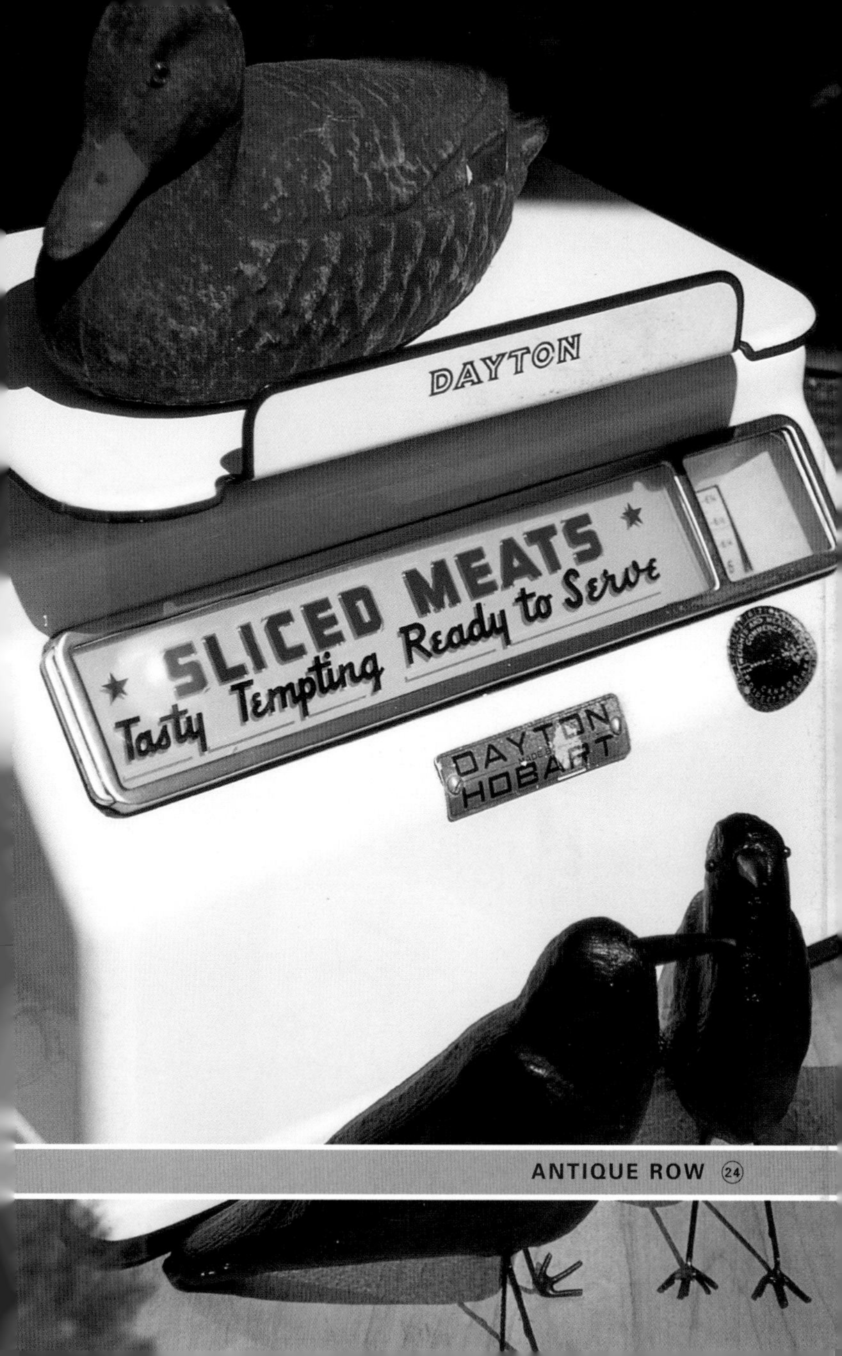

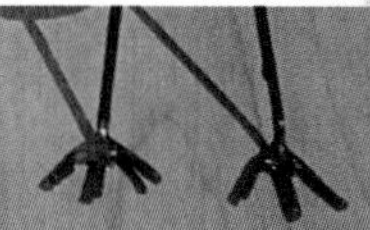

ANTIQUE ROW (24)

Main Street & Commercial Drive

WALKING TOUR 6

Take bus 3 toward Main and get off at East 28th Avenue. Cross the street and keep to the left. This is where the popular Antique Row begins (1), where you can visit countless antique shops. When you've had enough, go for lunch at The Reef (2), or to Locus (3) or Liberty Bakery (4). Afterwards, keep following Main Street (5). If you love antiques and art, you won't be able to skip this area. There are loads of nice stores opened by fashion designers and interior decorators (6) (7) (8) (9) (10) (11) (12). Turn left on East 14th Avenue and then right on Ontario Street. There are lovely residences on this street, but for something really special turn right on West 10th Avenue to have a look at the Davis Houses (13). Walk back to Manitoba Street and turn right; turn right on West Broadway for Vancouver's oldest skyscraper (14). At the corner of West Broadway and Main Street take bus 9 to Broadway Station and get out at the last stop (you can also keep walking if you prefer). Turn left at East Broadway and keep following the road until you get to Commercial Drive. Keep in mind that it will take at least half an hour. Turn left on Commercial Drive and walk under the bridge. Now you're on 'the Drive,' as the locals say. In the summer, people make full use of the many terraces and the small park at the end of the street. There are wonderful restaurants and many great places where you can go for coffee here (15) (16) (17) (18) (19) (20) (21) (22). Keep following Commercial Drive (23) (24) (25) (26) (27) (28) and end up at (29) where you can order a refreshing mojito and have a delicious meal!

Chinatown
Science World
SCIENCE WORLD / MAIN STREET
BROADWAY
NANAIMO
START
FINISH
E HASTINGS ST
E GEORGIA ST
DUNSMUIR ST
Pacific Blvd
Expo Blvd
MAIN ST
E BROADWAY
KINGSWAY
Grandview Hwy N
Grandview Hwy S
Great Northern Way
Terminal Ave
Industrial Ave
Malkin Ave
Commercial Dr
Victoria Dr
Nanaimo St
King Edward Ave E
Sights
Food & Drink
Shopping
Nice to do

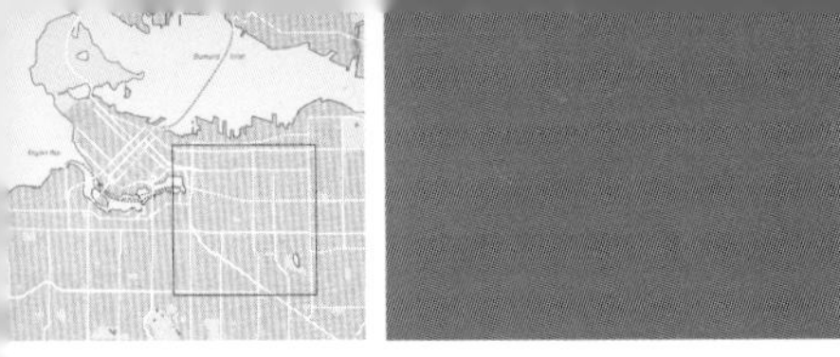

1 Antique Row
2 The Reef
3 Locus
4 Liberty Bakery
5 Homeworks
6 Front and Company
7 Simple
8 Smoking Lily
9 Eugene Choo
10 A Baker's Dozen
11 Starving Artist
12 Heritage Hall
13 Davis Houses
14 Lee Building
15 J.J. Bean House of Coffee
16 Café Deux Soleil
17 Clove
18 Belgian Fries
19 Wasubeez
20 Libra Room
21 Bukowski's
22 Fuse
23 Juicy Lucy's
24 Yogi's
25 Marcello
26 Dr. Vigari
27 Magpie
28 Turks
29 Havana's

Sights
Food & Drink
Shopping
Nice to do

Sights outside of the city center

The walking tours in this guide cover most of the sights in the city, but there are countless other sights worth seeing outside the center. Vancouver is connected to North and West Vancouver by two bridges, and these two areas offer interesting attractions and have their own characters. The atmosphere here is that of a quieter, family-oriented residential area.

A nice way to get from the North to the West and vice-versa is by seabus, a large ferry that takes you from one side to the other in about 20 minutes. You can find information about this ferry on the Vancouver Tourism Board's website, www.tourismvancouver.com.

A few sights not mentioned in the walking tours are highlighted below, the letters can be found on the map at the beginning of the guide.

(L) From downtown Vancouver it's only a 30-minute drive to some beautiful mountain areas. **Grouse Mountain** is one area particularly close to the city. Take a spectacular walk on the 'Grouse Grind' in the summer or go skiing in the winter. You can also take a cable car to the top of the mountain to enjoy the fantastic view.
6400 nancy greene way, telephone (604) 984-0661, www.grousemountain.com, open daily 9am-10pm, price cable car adults $24.95, children under 18 $13.95, bus 323 from phibbs exchange

(M) One of the most popular attractions in Vancouver is the **Capilano Suspension Bridge**. This enormous suspension bridge provides an adventurous crossing, wobbling high above the Capilano River. You can also enjoy the beautiful nature of Capilano Park.
3735 capilano road, telephone (604) 985-7474, www.capbridge.com, open daily winter 9am-5pm, summer 8.30am-dusk, price adults $14.95, children 12 and under $4, bus 247 from phibbs exchange

RIDGE
PREMIERE
INFO 738 6311
FIDEL
NIGHTLY 730 930
SUN MAT 530
PARKING
FIDEL

Ⓢ Vancouver's most popular club is the **Commodore Ballroom** where, in addition to disco nights on Tuesday (complete with 70s style costumes), there are regular concerts. If you want to go dancing, this is the place to be.
868 granville street, telephone (604) 739-4550, bus 8 granville

Ⓣ There's something different every night at the **Green Room**, including DJs, bands and an Open Mike Night - a great place to catch the first glimpse of up-and-coming musical talent.
695 cambie street, telephone (604) 608-2871, bus 17 cambie

Ⓤ The **Purple Onion** has something for everyone: two rooms for dancing to top-40 or DJ music, and a soulful lounge for a more relaxed evening.
15 water street, telephone (604) 602-9442, skytrain waterfront

Ⓥ The hippest people in Vancouver hang out at **Lucy Mae Brown's**. Not quite a dance club, this is a place to drink cocktails, have a bite to eat and meet interesting people.
862 richards street, telephone (604) 899-9199, bus 5 robson

Ⓦ On weekends, the **Roxy** fills up with young people looking to go wild. The music is different every night, but whatever is playing, you're guaranteed to have a good time.
932 granville street, telephone (604) 331-7999, bus 8 granville

Ⓧ Dance freaks will love **Sonar**, where the techno, trance and hip-hop beats will both challenge and inspire you.
66 water street, telephone (604) 683-6695, skytrain waterfront

Ⓨ The **Urban Well** is a small club, offering food as well as, on weekends, top-40 music to groove to on the small dance floor.
1516 yew street, telephone (604) 737-7770, bus 2 macdonald

Ⓩ Those in the know are aware that Vancouver's dance scene thrives underground... in the cellar of the Heritage Hotel. **The Lotus Sound Lounge** has a friendly atmosphere and plays hip-hop and techno music.
455 abbott street, telephone (604) 685-7777, bus 10 hastings

Alphabetical index

Category index

food & drink

sights

transportation

COLE HARBOUR

This guide has been compiled with the utmost care. Mo' Media BV cannot be held liable in the case of any inaccuracies within the text. Any remarks or comments should be directed to the following address.

mo' media, attn. 100% vancouver, p.o. box 7028,
4800 ga, breda, the netherlands, e-mail info@momedia.com

author	renske werner
translation	sushy mangat
final editing	zahra sethna & simon jones
photography	rebecca dadson
graphic design	www.studio100procent.nl, naarden
cartography	eurocartografie, hendrik-ido-ambacht
project guidance	joyce enthoven & sasja lagendijk, mo' media
printing office	south china printing co.

100% vancouver isbn 90 5767 116 6 - nur 510, 513

WWW.MOMEDIA.COM